W9-BAN-999

DAWN *of* *the* AKASHIC AGE

"*Dawn of the Akashic Age* is full of riveting ideas about the great evolutionary leap now facing humanity, but that is not what distinguishes this book. It is the masterful orchestration of leading-edge thinking into full symphonic resonance that sets it apart as a classic. It defines a new pinnacle of coherence in mapping our utter transformation as an evolved planetary species."

JAMES O'DEA, AUTHOR OF *CULTIVATING PEACE*,
FORMER PRESIDENT OF THE INSTITUTE OF NOETIC SCIENCES,
AND FORMER DIRECTOR OF THE WASHINGTON, D.C.,
OFFICE OF AMNESTY INTERNATIONAL

"In this remarkable book Laszlo and Dennis have done nothing less than draw the blueprint for a planetary society. The Akashic Age is the logical successor to both the Industrial Revolution and the Information Era, because it is based on a paradigm of connectedness not separation, of sustainability not exploitation, and of transformation not inertia. It serves as a healthy antidote to the doom and gloom found in most other books about humankind's future and warns that a positive transition and a better world will require deliberate effort, conscious deliberation, and hard work. Given the alternatives, readers of *Dawn of the Akashic Age* may decide that the required love and labor will be worth it."

STANLEY KRIPPNER, PH.D., PROFESSOR OF PSYCHOLOGY
AT SAYBROOK UNIVERSITY AND COAUTHOR OF
THE VOICE OF ROLLING THUNDER AND *HEALING STATES*

"Let it be said that a book has now been written about our future, a book that we ignore at our peril. This inspiring book is the alarm clock that can stir us from our slumber."

LARRY DOSSEY, M.D., AUTHOR OF *ONE MIND* AND *HEALING WORDS* AND FORMER EXECUTIVE EDITOR OF *ALTERNATIVE THERAPIES IN HEALTH AND MEDICINE*

DAWN *of the* AKASHIC AGE

NEW CONSCIOUSNESS, QUANTUM RESONANCE, AND THE FUTURE OF THE WORLD

Ervin Laszlo
and
Kingsley L. Dennis

Inner Traditions
Rochester, Vermont • Toronto, Canada

Inner Traditions
One Park Street
Rochester, Vermont 05767
www.InnerTraditions.com

Text stock is SFI certified

Copyright © 2013 by Ervin Laszlo and Kingsley L. Dennis

All rights reserved. No part of this book may be reproduced or utilized in any form or by any means, electronic or mechanical, including photocopying, recording, or by any information storage and retrieval system, without permission in writing from the publisher.

Library of Congress Cataloging-in-Publication Data
Laszlo, Ervin, 1932–
  Dawn of the akashic age : new consciousness, quantum resonance, and the future of the world / Ervin Laszlo and Kingsley L. Dennis.
      pages cm
  Includes bibliographical references and index.
  Summary: "A preview of the post-mechanistic, holistic world in 2020 and 2030 as well as a map of the obstacles we must overcome to get there"—Provided by publisher.
  ISBN 978-1-62055-104-2 (print) — ISBN 978-1-62055-152-3 (e-book)
  1. Civilization—Forecasting. 2. Future, The. 3. Spiritual life—Miscellanea. I. Dennis, Kingsley. II. Title.
  CB161.L366 2013
  303.49—dc23
                                                                          2012045058

Printed and bound in the United States by Lake Book Manufacturing, Inc. The text stock is SFI certified. The Sustainable Forestry Initiative® program promotes sustainable forest management.

10 9 8 7 6 5 4 3 2 1

Text design by Jon Desautels and layout by Brian Boynton
This book was typeset in Garamond Premier Pro with Goudy Old Style and Copperplate as display typefaces

To send correspondence to the authors of this book, mail a first-class letter to the authors c/o Inner Traditions • Bear & Company, One Park Street, Rochester, VT 05767, and we will forward the communication, or contact the authors directly at **www.kingsleydennis.com** for Kingsley Dennis and **http://ervinlaszlo.com** for Ervin Laszlo.

CONTENTS

INTRODUCTION
RISING TO A NEW DAWN

At first glance it may seem ambitious to name a book the *dawn* of something; more so when it heralds the dawn of what is called an Akashic Age. What do we mean when we refer to an age that is "Akashic"? The ancient *rishis* of India believed that beyond the four elements of the cosmos—fire, water, air, and earth—there is a fifth element that is more fundamental than all the others: the *Akasha*. The *Akasha* is the fundamental dimension of the world, a dimension that has been rediscovered at the cutting edge of contemporary physics and cosmology, where it is called variously Unified Field, nu-ether, cosmic matrix, or physical space-time. The *Akasha* thus heralds a dimension that is our fundamental underlying connectivity, one that is now being verified by our new sciences. The subtitle of this book, too, speaks of a new consciousness, quantum resonance, and the future of the world. You might be asking, Is this too far-fetched? Naturally, we—the authors—think not. Furthermore, we feel that not only is such a future possible, but that it is the natural developmental progression of a global civilization that is on the cusp of becoming a planetary society. However, we are aware that this is not a simple process. Nor is it likely to be a thoroughly smooth transition. Hence, the need for this book to further elucidate just what is meant by arriving at an interrelated, integral, and interdependent planetary society.

Our species, *Homo sapiens sapiens,* has been on a historically long evolutionary journey prior to arriving at the point where we now find ourselves. Thus we begin our book by offering an—albeit brief—examination of the rise of hominid intelligence. Within this context we acknowledge that to arrive at a world that is complex and interdependent, by making the right type of choices, is hard, but critical. Whereas previously we perhaps had the luxury of making choices that affected only our immediate well-being and locale, we must now think and act in a global context and with a long time horizon. We feel it is important to be clear on this matter: we are approaching a crucial epoch that will serve as a cusp in our species development. We are leaving behind one age and entering the next. The epoch we are leaving behind is the Modern Age. The epoch we are about to shift into has been given many names—Postmodern, Digital, and the like—yet has so far suffered from lack of true and genuine foresight. Partly to blame is the human inclination to think in linear terms, and thus to imagine the future as a logical extension of the past. We see it as a gradual upward sloping curve on a graph. But nature—and evolution—doesn't work that way, and never has. What we see are long periods of static where there is relatively little change; then the onset of a tipping point where a crucial—and critical—leap occurs. What is on the other side of this leap is often unexpected, because it does not conform to the older patterns of thinking, perception, and behavior. These periods of criticality are moments of opportunity, when catalysts for change exert a greater than normal influence on the outcome of events. It is a transition period where the anomalies begin to manifest at the periphery and witness the implosion of the incumbent status quo. At these points, ideas, institutions, and beliefs tend to outlive their usefulness.

Yet there are guiding principles that can help us, if not to predict the future, then at least to foresee alternative models of the future. Our view is that the systems sciences enable us to do just that—to view underlying trends that flow through the veins of biological as well as sociocultural evolution. To put it simply, the systems that arise and evolve—corporeal, environmental, social systems—veer toward ever-increasing size and complexity. We are embedded within systems that seek growth through increasing complexity and numerous levels of organization, greater dynamism, and closer interaction and more delicate balance with the environment. We foresee a future that is highly connected and integrated, more decentralized, technologically advanced, more sustainably balanced, and nonlocally interconnected. By *nonlocally* interconnected, we mean that physical objects/bodies—as well as human consciousness—maintain effective forms of relationships at a distance. The term *nonlocality* comes to us from the quantum sciences, which are central to offering the world a new paradigm of inclusive, intrinsic, and immediate oneness. It is a paradigm that helps to explain how we are all connected through fields of energy, which forms a basis for the continued physical proximity and connectivity that develops in the world. This emerging new paradigm is the key in understanding what we are calling the Akashic Age.

Is this still far-fetched? Well, for us, it is entirely scientific; that is, within the domain of science and scientific validity. The new sciences, based on the physics of the quantum, show us that this wonderful world of ours is a gigantic macro-level quantum system, where all things, and not only supersmall quantum things, are entangled; that is, instantly interconnected. As we discuss in the book, this realization is set to change our values and aspirations, and the very way we think and act in the world. It may hold the key to our own well-being, and the survival of the whole human community. As we state in part 1, a sustainable global civilization *could* come about, and if it did, its advent would be in tune with the overall trend in the evolution of complex systems. Thus, we envision that a positive unfolding of the sociocultural evolutionary trend is definitely possible. But bringing it about depends on us: on what we do today, and in the years ahead.

We are at the dawn of the Akashic Age because there remain a number of dilemmas and critical thresholds that we face. We see these as potential opportunities as well as potential disrupters. They will unfold over the next decade. Significantly, we view them as being based, to a large degree, on energy, communications, and consciousness. We refer to energy in terms of how we utilize our resources, communications in terms of how we connect and collaborate with each other, and consciousness in terms of our patterns of thinking and inner coherence.

As we approach the Akashic Age, we are entering a time of transition, where our crises become our catalysts, and our disruptions become our driving forces. In such times, when there are major fluctuations in worldviews, values, and beliefs, we are compelled to reorganize how we think about and do things. Such moments are ripe for new models to emerge. These new models are likely to first emerge on the periphery—as anomalies—before creeping toward the center to overwhelm and outdo the centralized and self-centered old systems. These new models also display a marked difference from their predecessors in that they operate through decentralized and distributed channels, as horizontal networks of connection and collaboration, rather than as the vertical, top-down hierarchical systems of control in the old systems. Whereas previous models of civilization continued to grow through increasing centralization and hierarchy, they have now entered history with a death cry and the onset of final collapse.

For our planet to have any future that is not only sustainable but also fosters human developmental growth and well-being, we need an Akashic Age that promotes the natural, integrated flow of living systems. Such an age, as we foresee it, encourages social as well as self-actualization, and plants the seeds of a new culture that respects and honors the Earth and her diverse peoples. The Akashic Age represents a new stage in human consciousness, a stage that allows humanity to rise and overcome all the challenges we now confront. We ask you, the reader, to join us on this journey, and to envision the possibility that such an age may be more than just a possible future. It can be *our* future, if we truly want it to be.

■ ■ ■

In part 1 of this book, "Our Path to the Akashic Age," we examine the evolutionary journey of *Homo sapiens sapiens* and how we have arrived at our current stage. We ask the question *What next?* as we discuss the dilemmas that now face us as we stand at a historical turning point.

Part 2, "At the Threshold of the Akashic Age," looks at how we can shift our values and beliefs. In this section we introduce the background to the new quantum sciences that underlie the Akashic paradigm and that foster qualities of coherence and quantum resonance. With this in mind, we introduce to the reader our vision of what an Akashic dawn could look like, with new emerging models in society, energy, economics, food production, and education, among other things.

Part 3, "The Conscious Advent of the Akashic Age," takes this vision further to consider what a world of 2030 might have in store for us if we were to follow the Akashic path. With this vision, we take the opportunity to put forth what we consider to be the Manifesto of a New Consciousness, which suggests fifteen points to guide our steps as we seek a higher consciousness to live and thrive on this planet.

Finally, part 4, "From Vision to Reality," offers a rich set of future-visioning contributions from the world-shifting community on such issues as spirituality, education, social entrepreneurship, conscious leadership, and sacred economics.

As philosopher Arthur Schopenhauer once famously said, "Everyone takes the limits of his own vision for the limits of the world." It is time now to throw off these limits, and together provide this wonderful world with the vision of a future that lives up to the true potential of a species endowed with higher purpose and consciousness.

PART ONE

Our Path to the
Akashic Age

1

HOW WE BECAME *SAPIENS*

Homo sapiens no longer rely on the muscle of fight, the speed of flight, or the protective mask of shape and coloring for survival. We have come to depend on our intelligence. We evolved into *Homo sapiens,* subspecies *sapiens,* doubly man the knower. But do we live up to this proud designation?

About 5 million years ago, the evolutionary line that led to modern humanity diverged from African apes, the common ancestors of humans, chimpanzees, and gorillas. Apes are knuckle-walking quadrupeds; *Homo* is an erect biped. Apes have large jaws and they have small brains (in the range of 300–600 cubic centimeters [ccm]); *Homo* has a small jaw and a fourfold brain size, in the range of 1400–1600 ccm. Most apes are adapted to life in the trees; *Homo* is suited to life on the ground. It is this adaptability to terrestrial life that proved to be the decisive factor in the evolution of intelligence. Why some bands of prehominids left the trees is still something of a mystery (some anthropologists maintain that they were pushed from the forests into the savannah by physically more developed arboreal primates), but once they left the trees, their destiny was sealed: they were condemned to a form of intelligence—or to extinction. The question we now face is whether the kind of intelligence that evolved is sufficient for survival into the twenty-first century. Humanity, as Buckminster Fuller said, is facing its final exam. It is an exam of intelligence—the collective IQ test of the species.

Intelligence in a species is not unique to *Homo*—other animals have developed forms of it, and more species might have developed it, if they had had the need and the opportunity to do so. Whales and dolphins have intelligence, but they live in an aquatic environment that is more stable and more readily able to satisfy the requirements of living beings than life on land. Sea mammals had no need to evolve into the kind of active, manipulative intelligent beings that land-living humans did. This kind of intelligence is needed only in a terrestrial setting, where the availability and retention of water, continual energy storage and usage, and the maintenance of constant temperatures are essential to the running of complex biochemical reactions. A corresponding kind of intelligence may have emerged in various land-living species; in time it may have emerged among the dinosaurs. One species, the stenanicosaurus, had favorable prerequisites—a spacious cranium, large eyes, and long arms—but it disappeared along with the rest. Had stenanicosaurus evolved with a high level of intelligence, the biosphere might now be populated by reptilian rather than human beings, with (for us) mind-boggling consequences.

Unlike the history of dinosaurs and sea-living mammals, the chance concatenation of circumstances that made up the history of our own species allowed, and even required, our ancestors to stake their survival on a form of intelligence that was able to adapt quickly and to manipulate its surroundings. The gamble had to be taken because, once they were out of the trees, our forebears found themselves in a perilous situation. The savannahs were already populated with meat-eating animals, most of them stronger and faster than our ancesters were. The shelter of the trees was gone, and in its place they had only one substitute: their newly freed forelimbs. These were no longer needed to hold on to the branches of trees and could thus be put to other uses. Most probably, the evolving arms were used to transport infants as the bands of early hominids followed migrating herds on Africa's developing grasslands. But they must also have been used for self-defense with stones and sticks, as chimpanzees use their forelimbs. Unlike in chimps and other apes, however, our forebears' method of survival put a premium on bodily control, tactile sensitivity, and especially on manual dexterity. Only hominids who evolved these capabilities could survive. Our early ancestors managed this feat: in the motor and sensory cortex of the brain of *sapiens*, the nerves governing the hand, especially the thumb, became highly developed.

As forelimbs morphed into dexterous arms and hands, jaws were no longer required for defense. There was no selection pressure for canine teeth, sectorial premolars, or a capacious jaw to accommodate them. The pressure was for a bigger brain, capable of dexterity and intelligence, and for a cranium to shelter it. Hence, an erect bipedal species arose, with a large brain, a small jaw, and opposable thumbs—the hallmarks of *sapiens* to this day.

With the development of a larger brain came a whole series of evolutionary innovations. Among the capabilities that were advantageous to terrestrial bipeds, the ability to cooperate in performing the critical tasks of survival must have been the foremost. Mutant individuals who had a superior ability to communicate with each other were most likely favored by natural selection. As these socialized individuals spread through the population, the genetically based sign language of the apes morphed into the flexible system of shared symbols characteristic of human language. Social behavior was freed from the rigidity of genetic programming and adapted to changing circumstances. In the neocortex, the capacities for manual dexterity and tool use were joined with newly evolved capacities for communication and socialization. Our forebears evolved from terrestrial apes into a species that, with some exaggeration but not entirely without reason, came to view itself as the "knower."

Sapiens remained essentially unchanged since the species first emerged in Africa about 100,000 years ago. But its sophisticated manual and cognitive capacities did not pay off during the greater part of the 5 million years since our forebears first descended from the trees. During most of these thousands of millennia, the scattered bands of hominids just scraped by, barely surviving in a world that was always vulnerable and frequently precarious.

The payoffs began slowly, perhaps 1.5 million years ago. Near Chesowanja in Kenya, archaeologists have found baked clay next to hominid bones and human-made stone implements. The clay showed traces of exposure to heat much higher than that which would normally occur in a bush fire. Whether it had been baked by fires tended by hominids who lived 1.5 million years ago is uncertain; the evidence is circumstantial—natural fires leading to an intense smoldering of a big tree trunk could have produced similarly high temperatures. But 500,000 years back in time, the evidence becomes uncontroversial. Fires of human origin are at least as old as that—and that is perhaps the first indication that our species's gamble on intelligence would eventually pay off.

The control of fire was an intelligent move: it gave the dispersed bands of hominids a small but decisive edge in their struggle for survival. Fire inspires fear in all creatures—flames and embers burn feathers, fur, hair, and skin on contact. Since the instinctive reaction to fire is to flee, those who master fire can use it for protection and defense. Fire is also an important aid in ensuring a continuous food supply; meat that quickly rots when raw remains edible far longer when it's properly roasted. By roasting the food, lean periods between hunts in poor weather can be bridged; one is no longer living entirely from hand to mouth.

Mastering fire, the most immediate and fearful of all elementary forces of nature, is not likely to have come about all at once, and in one place only. *Homo erectus,* our direct forebear, seems to have tended fires in far-distant locations over long periods. The finds speak clearly: there were humanly laid fires at such diverse sites as Zhoukoudian near Beijing, Aragon in the south of France, and Vértesszöllôs in Hungary. A number of hominid bands seem to have mastered fire almost simultaneously, without learning from, or probably even knowing about, each other.

The process must have been slow, at least by modern standards. There are fires ignited periodically by lightning in all tropical and subtropical ecosystems. Natural fires play a vital role: they clear away dead organic matter and revitalize the soil, creating favorable conditions for fresh plant growth. *Homo erectus* certainly encountered natural fires for untold millennia and, most likely, reacted much the same as other apes and animals—by fleeing. But gradually, some adventuresome individuals were drawn back to the smoldering remains and began to poke around in them. No doubt, they discovered the remains of many kinds of animals, and found some that were charred but not entirely burned. Experience might have shown them that such remains could be eaten, not only at the site of the fire, but at home bases for days afterward.

More and more of the exploring hominid bands undoubtedly returned to the sites of natural fires to forage for edible remains. They would not have been the only ones to do so: other animals, especially the readily imitating apes and monkeys, would have followed suit. But hominids had an advantage: with their thinly haired bodies they were less likely to be singed by flying sparks than more furry or hairy animals. Their erect posture was even more of an advantage. Liberated arms could be used far better to investigate embers and ashes than the forelimbs of quadrupeds; in addition, they could be used more effectively to hurl stones and sticks at competitors.

Then a whole series of discoveries occurred. First, some hominids noticed that a stick that smolders or burns on one end is cool enough to be handled on the other. They found that such sticks make particularly effective weapons. Entire bands of hominids rallied, making noises and brandishing burning sticks to frighten off other animals. Another discovery was made subsequently: some individuals threw dry sticks on the flames, and made handy torches for use as a weapon.

The act of igniting the end of a dry stick marked a decisive breakthrough in our species's gamble on intelligence. A natural fire goes out after a time, but one that is kindled with additional sticks keeps burning. Our ancestors discovered that, by lighting sticks, they could not only frighten off other animals but could keep fires going. Since natural fires would not occur at all times—periods without lightning can be long—keeping fires burning became an important chore.

And then a third discovery was made: fire could be transported. A burning stick could be carried and made to ignite fires at more convenient locations, for example, in or near caves. Fires were then built near human habitations and were used for roasting food as well as for keeping predators at bay. There is evidence that fires were indeed used in this way, and for staggering periods. The famous cave at Zhoukoudian, for example, seems to have had a fire that was tended off and on for about 230,000 years—and was abandoned only when the roof collapsed and the cave had to be vacated.

Through the centuries, hominids have discovered that they could make fires on their own, without having to wait for the serendipity of a bolt of lightning igniting dry bush. Rubbing together sticks and stones and blowing on the sparks was a remarkable discovery by hominid intelligence. Together with the earlier discoveries, it endowed our ancestors with a significant measure of control over nature, far more than any other creature.

With this discovery, our species acquired an assured path to dominance. Humans no longer had to struggle for survival in constant fear of more powerful species: they could establish habitations, protect them, and stockpile their staple foods. A Greek myth tells us that Prometheus stole the fire withheld by an avenging Zeus, angry at humans for having gotten the better of him. The Promethean spark, concealed according to legend in the hollow stalk of a fennel, may have been the greatest breakthrough in the history of *sapiens*.

With the edge on survival assured, the payoffs of intelligence accumulated at an increasing rate. River valleys, such as the Nile, the Tigris, the Euphrates, the Ganges, and the Huang-Ho, were settled. In these environments, silt deposited by great streams acted as a natural fertilizer, and periodically flooding waters functioned as natural systems of irrigation. In the course of millennia, regular harvests were supplemented by seeds planted on favorable locations; several strains of previously wild plants could be successfully domesticated. The domestication of a few species of animals occurred at more or less the same time. With the advent of the Neolithic Age (circa 10,000 BCE)—a breakthrough that has a rightful claim to be the first great technological "revolution"—the nomadic bands of hominids morphed into settled pastoralists.

The rest is indeed history—the history of *sapiens,* the dominant predator of this planet. The intelligence we evolved permitted us to reproduce in ever-greater numbers and to dominate—or at least to interfere with—nature, according to the dictates of our growing needs and our increasingly voracious appetites.

BUT ARE WE REALLY *SAPIENS*?

We have learned to make fire and have acted on the assumption that we can also put it out. But is such confidence justified? The forces we have called into being are all fires of one kind or another—dynamic processes in nature that we catalyze and then hope to control. We believe that we have tamed these Promethean fires, that we cannot only create them but can also extinguish them at will. Yet some of the fires we have sparked get out of hand occasionally. Some, like a maverick genie let out of a bottle, take on a life and will of their own. They act in unforeseen and unintended ways, destroying rather than building life and habitat. This was how the force we liberated with the invention of gunpowder behaved, and how most of our fossil fuel–based technologies behave today. As Hiroshima, Chernobyl, and, more recently, Fukushima taught us, the genie we have let out of the nucleus of the atom is more powerful and more difficult to tame than all the others. Robots, computers, and the myriad new technologies of automation and communication we have come up with may not turn out to be reliably domesticated, either.

All this should give us pause. When the line of *Homo* branched off from the higher apes some 5 million years ago, our species—and with it terrestrial nature—took a chance. It put its own survival at stake. An intelligent species is not necessarily an evolutionary success, reproducing and enhancing its environment. It might also be an ecological disaster, degrading its milieu and threatening its own survival. If human intelligence were to end in a fiasco, the exit of our species could ignite a "fire" that destroys the habitat for all higher forms of life on the planet. The bet on intelligence is the greatest gamble the biosphere has ever entered into.

Though the outcome was in doubt for millions of years, in the span of recorded history the bet seems to have paid off. Yet, could it be that this period in history is now coming to an end? To envision the extinction of our species is by no means far-fetched: elsewhere in the universe, intelligent species may have disappeared not long after they became dominant. Intelligence, after all, is one of the many answers that evolution can offer in the great dance of mutation and natural selection, and it is likely that in the wide reaches of the universe similar answers will have been chanced upon. Despite this, our efforts at interplanetary communication have been a failure. There have been reports of UFOs with extraterrestrials on board landing on Earth, but they are not confirmed and their veracity has been questioned.

Even though there are many planets capable of supporting life within communication range from Earth, we have not established regular contact with any of them. The reason may not be that intelligent species do not exist beyond our planet, but that, even if a few may be interspersed in the galaxy, such species do not survive for long. If most of them have a short life expectancy, our chances of communicating with them are drastically reduced. We would have to be precisely coordinated in space and time to receive signals from them: a few hundred years too soon and they would not be capable of emitting the signals; a few hundred years too late and they would no longer be there to emit them.

Whether or not it exists elsewhere in the cosmos, we pride ourselves that intelligent life exists here on Earth. But does it? The answer depends on the meaning we attach to *intelligence*. As a strategy for competitive survival, intelligence of the human kind does exist: it has paid off handsomely in the last few thousand years. Yet its costs have been rising and now threaten to supersede its benefits. If they do, our species will turn into a planetary parasite that kills the host on which it feeds, a kind of cancer that destroys the biosphere. And that would hardly be intelligent—deserving to be called *sapiens sapiens*.

2

WHAT NEXT?

It could still turn out that *Homo* is *sapiens sapiens*. Being sapient—intelligent—means having the ability to make considered choices. In a world that is complex and interdependent, making such choices is not easy. It calls for thinking and acting in a global context, with a long time horizon. Short-range tunnel vision could prove fatal: it may lead to choices that prove disastrous for the individual who makes them and catastrophic for the environment in which that species has evolved.

Will our intelligence test out in the end; that is, will we make the right choices? This is the ultimate question. Our collective survival depends on it. When a Stone Age fire got out of hand, part of the forest or savannah was destroyed and some habitations had to be vacated, so the nomadic bands of *sapiens* living there moved to untouched regions. Throughout the Modern Age, "Go West, young man" was a feasible proposition—one could always set out for as-yet-virgin lands. But today the situation is altogether different. The forces humanity is now unleashing do not leave any region of this planet untouched: if they get out of hand, there will be nowhere left to go. If we make the wrong choices, we will use our megatechnologies to dig a megagrave for ourselves.

We are approaching a crucial epoch: a cusp in our species development. We are leaving behind one age and entering the next. The epoch we are leaving behind is the Modern Age. The one we are entering most people know only as the Postmodern Age—although some speculate that it will be the Digital Age, the Ecological Age, or the Integral Age. What will that epoch or age really be like?

The drive to identify the age or epoch that comes after the modern one runs up against a major problem: that of seeing into the future. Gone are the days when people could content themselves with consulting sages, astrologers, and soothsayers; tea leaves, horoscopes, and crystal balls tend to become fuzzy when it comes to answering queries about the future of humanity. Social scientists, too, seem reluctant to commit themselves. Why? Because in the standard branches of the social sciences, one can read and extrapolate trends, provided the parameters are constant and the epoch itself is stable, but not if the rules of the game themselves change. Periods of fundamental change bedevil the calculations, and often those making them.

We need to respond to some basic questions. Can we predict the human future? And, if so, within what limits? The limits of predictability in the human sphere may not be the same as those that apply to simpler systems. Take a well-wound clock, for example. Its hands move across the dial face with strict regularity. If we know where the hands are now, we shall know where they will be five minutes, one hour, or twenty-four hours from now. Also, the movement of the planets in the solar system is, for all intents and purposes, regular and dependable, and, hence, predictable. But the "movement" of humanity through history may not be as predictable as that. We could question whether it is predictable at all.

The human future is predictable if the past is—that is, if there are laws or regularities that have determined the course of history. Could there be such laws, and, if there are, what are they?

Two kinds of laws might come into play here. One pertains to the nature of the human organism; the other to the nature of societies. The former set of laws or factors is biological; if it is determinant, it would create a form of biological (or, more precisely, genetic) determinism. The latter set is sociological, and, if determinant, it would, in turn, spell societal (that is, sociocultural or civilizational) determinism. Let us look at each in turn.

BIOLOGICAL EVOLUTION

If biological factors determined the course of history, they would also determine the future. Our history, the same as our destiny, would be decided by the biological evolution of our species. Our future would be more or less unchanged if our species remained unchanged, and different if our species changed—that is, if it evolved into another species or subspecies.

This viewpoint accords with a reputable school of thought that looks at the information encoded in our genes as the ultimate determinant of behavior. Sociobiology, as developed in the 1970s by Harvard biologist E. O. Wilson, produced an impressive array of evidence. Sociobiology's central principle is that individuals tend to behave in a manner that maximizes their inclusive fitness. "Fitness" is measured by reproduction, by the success of individuals in projecting copies of themselves—more precisely, of their genes—into succeeding generations. Genes, according to biologist Richard Dawkins, are "selfish"; that is, their sole purpose is to reproduce themselves. The complexities of the human body and of human behavior are the only means to achieve this paramount end.

If we press the argument to its logical conclusion, even social interactions appear largely determined by our genes. Other than the embellishment of this or that function through the creation of this or that social structure, human society is as much the expression of the genetic endowment of its members as an animal or insect society is. We may think that we live in societies freely created by us; in reality, we live in superanthills and ultrabeehives in which the complexities of structure and function are due mainly to our own genetic makeup. Our genes make us egotistical: social structure is the result of a trade-off between the selfish aims of individuals and the recognition that many of these aims can be better served by joining forces than by going it alone. Our genes make us aggressive: the history of societies is the history of wars, only interspersed by the cessation of hostilities because periodically there is a need to recoup one's strength and regroup one's forces. Our genes make us thirst for power: the structures of society are the product of the power struggle of individuals as the stronger subdue and bind the weaker. The basic traits of individual human behavior are all mirrored by corresponding characteristics in society.

The conclusion one is tempted to draw from this view is that human society is unlikely to change in the near future. People will be selfish, aggressive, power-seeking tomorrow, just as they are today. There will be wars, power plays, and other conflict-driven behaviors in the future as well. Human society, like the human body, is the way it is because human genes are the way they are. As long as our genes remain the same, society remains the same. No hope for a different future, at least not in the span of the next few generations. It would take a new human to make a new society, and the new human awaits a new mutation in the gene pool of the human species.

There have been many dreams of creating a new and superior human being; they have ranged from Friedrich Nietzsche's *Übermensch* and Adolf Hitler's Teutonic superman to more recent speculations concerning the attempt to control human breeding stocks through eugenics. The Nazi regime attempted to spread the Aryan stock widely and eliminate what it considered inferior breeds, such as Gypsies, Jews, and Slavs. Extermination camps that put the worst excesses of the medieval Inquisition to shame were the means of accomplishing this "final solution."

More well-meaning champions of genetic engineering speak of the elimination of deficient traits by splicing the amino-acid sequences that make up the genetic code of individuals. They hope that laboratories could produce a species genetically superior to today's *sapiens,* with traits such as greater intellectual ability; less proneness to aggression, fear, and rage; less susceptibility to disease; and greater tolerance of a wider range of climates and environments.

The prospect appears promising. Through careful genetic manipulation, controlled interbreeding, and the selective diffusion of the new stock, we could mutate *sapiens* to a higher form. We could breed *Homo supersapiens,* whose selfish traits would be balanced by genes coding for sociability, whose aggression would be kept in check by an instinct for belongingness, and whose hunger for power would be mitigated by a genetic disposition for cooperation. *Supersapiens* may not need a larger cranium and bigger brain than today's *sapiens:* it would be enough for *supersapiens* to use more of their brain. Intelligent, sociable, and cooperative, *supersapiens* would create a new society and usher in a new age.

New genes, a new humanity, and a new society—all made to order. The concept may be attractive; the more is the pity that it is hopelessly unrealistic. Why so?

First, because it turns out that specific DNA sequences do not produce corresponding personality traits. Genes are only the basic switches operated by adaptive and manipulative systems in the individual. The living state is maintained by epigenetic, and not directly genetic, regulation. A system of regulation within the organism activates and deactivates the genetic endowment of the species to meet the survival needs of the individual organism. Experiments show that epigenetic self-regulation has long-standing effects: it can even be handed down to succeeding generations.

Second, even if we assumed that we could accelerate the evolutionary process by deliberate and purposeful intervention, we would still have to count on at least thirty generations passing before a mutant gene could diffuse and define the dominant traits of the human species. This would give us an evolutionary leap of some six thousand years, far too long to be relevant to our own common future. When confronted with these realities, the dream of creating the future by creating the "new person" soon evaporates.

In any case, creating individual personality traits would not be enough: we would also have to legitimize the emerging traits, ensuring that individuals possessing them could reproduce and spread them throughout the population. In the absence of a radical intervention in the normal processes of society, the "new person" with a hyperintellectual and nonaggressive disposition would soon end up in the dustbin of history, eliminated in the competition with more egotistical and aggressive specimens. The latter would breed on, making more of their selfish and aggressive kind.

It does not matter in the least that we cannot mutate our species as we would like. The kind of change we need in the future is not the kind that our good *sapiens* stock would be unable to produce. We have been essentially the same genetic individuals for the past 100,000 years and, except for straightening our posture, reducing the size of our jaw, increasing the size of our brain, and developing a better gripping hand (and less well-gripping feet), we have not been very different for the past 5 million years. Genetically, we are surprisingly close to the higher apes and almost identical with a whole series of previous hominid types—no specimen of which would we enjoy having as our next-door neighbor.

There has been a complex series of different cultural types in the history of *Homo sapiens*. Only three thousand years have elapsed since the advent of *Homo classicus*, one thousand years since the emergence of *Homo medievalis*, and four hundred years since *Homo modernus*. Each of these cultural types created a different age, even if their genes were the same—for it is not genes that determine the nature of an age. The genetic heritage of *sapiens* is generous enough to give rise to many scores of ages and societies, several times more than those that have come about in our history. *Homo modernus* could be followed by many different varieties of *Homo postmodernus*.

One day, probably in the as-yet-distant future, our species may very well mutate biologically. But we should hold off trying to create a major mutation: that way is filled with danger. A major mutation has such a high probability of depressing the viability of a species as to amount to a near-certainty. Only a long process of natural selection can weed out the unfit mutants and find that small fraction that has enhanced viability. Intentional, technologically driven intervention cannot be sure to produce a viable mutation. All intentional interference with the human gene pool—even those who seek the elimination of so-called genetic defects—entails grave dangers and is rightfully viewed with suspicion.

However, there could also be unintentional, accidental mutations. The threat of an accidental mutation is real—as real as that of any other technological catastrophe. Today, with the higher radiation levels to which we are exposed; the huge amount of airborne pollutants we breathe in; the chemicals we consume in our food; and all the synthetics we're exposed to, even in our clothing, our gene pool is seriously under attack. Experiments show that genetic changes can and do result from radiation and unnatural living conditions. They could result from the conditions to which we are exposed in our lifetime.

While we do not know how to create a desirable mutation, we could well create an undesirable one—entirely inadvertently.

If accidental mutations occurred in large numbers, the human gene pool would soon be severely contaminated. Future generations would be born with defective genes; they would have less resistance to disease, a shorter life span, and fewer children. For all intents and purposes, the effects would be irreversible: we would not know how to regenerate our present characteristics. The conclusion is obvious: we should let biological evolution be. We should not strive to create intentional mutations, and avert the specter of accidental ones.

But we need not grieve over our inability to create a genetically new human. What we need is not a biologically, but a socially, culturally, and civilizationally new human.

SOCIOCULTURAL EVOLUTION

What about social, or more precisely sociocultural, civilizational evolution: is it predictable or not?

Few people would agree that society is as determined as the hands of a clock. There are, however, other kinds and degrees of determinism, and just how, and to what extent, society may be determined is the subject of lively debate. On one side are the philosophers and social theorists who believe that society is governed by "iron laws"—laws of history that will determine its future as they have determined its past. On the other side are thinkers and scientists who go as far as to deny any kind and degree of determinism in regard to society. Far from moving ahead on a predetermined trajectory, like the hands of a clock, society has no trajectory but makes its way through chance and circumstance.

Let us look at the determinist hypothesis first. The future of society is predictable if there are determining factors of sociocultural evolution and we know what they are. These factors could be iron laws, natural principles, or even the will of God. We could know them through the empirical method of science, through mystical intuition, or through religious revelation. All that counts is that the determinant factors should exist and be knowable. If we know what they are, we can predict the future.

Determinism of this kind lands us in a fatalistic frame of mind. The future will be what it will be; as a once popular song had it, *"Que sera, sera."* We may want to know what the next year or the next century will bring, but this interest will stem more from curiosity than from a desire to master our destiny. Predicting the future will be like solving a crossword puzzle: the solution exists already; the task is just to find it.

Yet predictability of a complete, fatalistic kind is hardly ever affirmed in the sciences and only seldom in the world's religions. Almost always some leeway is allowed for conscious and purposeful action—for intervention even in an otherwise deterministic process. Even Marxist doctrine, the radically deterministic theory of historical materialism, held that intentional human action could influence the course of events. And non-Marxist doctrines are far less deterministic than that.

Most scientists agree that what people do could be decisive in creating a different kind of society. This does not necessarily mean creating it consciously. History is full of surprises, with people creating changed conditions beyond the ability of anyone to foresee them. Tsarist Russia yielded to the Bolshevik ideology, even though Russia was not a bourgeois society and had no proletariat to speak of—not to mention a historically conscious one. The intellectually sophisticated Germany of the Weimar Republic gave rise to Hitler, even though Nazi slogans and theories bordered on the insane. The shah of Iran, Mohammad Reza Pahlavi, the self-styled king of kings with a powerful military and vast police machinery at his command, fled before the followers of an aged and exiled Islamic fundamentalist. And the same kind of surprise occurred in Fulgencio Battista's Cuba, Ferdinand Marcos's Philippines, and the wild swings of allegiance in Ethiopia and Benin, to mention only a few of the major "surprises" of the past hundred years. Historians did not predict and politicians did not anticipate these and similar events.

Yet the fact that unexpected events occur at times does not mean that we must renounce the idea that history follows laws of its own. The surprises could, after all, be due to our ignorance of the laws. Moreover, there could be laws that do not strictly determine what will happen, but offer only probabilities and indicate overall trends. Such nondeterministic (so-called stochastic) laws are known in natural science—physics would be lost without them—and they are likely to hold true in the human sphere as well. There could be a pattern in history, even if it doesn't unfold in fully deterministic ways.

Systems sciences—the study of how systems operate in nature, society, and science—do find an overall pattern in history, and can extrapolate it into the future without claiming certitude for it: the extrapolation is probabilistic and not deterministic. We are dealing with trends, not rigorously deterministic processes. The basic trend can be spelled out: according to the systems sciences, it is toward societies of increasing size and complexity, of increasingly high and numerous levels of social organization, of greater dynamism, and of closer interaction with the environment.

If these trends hold true, postmodern society could approximate current notions of an integral, connected age: it could be globally integrated, technologically advanced, and nonlocally entangled. Human settlements will be organized on multiple levels, from the grass roots of villages, farming communities, and urban neighborhoods, through townships, districts, provinces, national and federated states, all the way to the global community as a whole. Each level will be coordinated with all the others. And the globally integrated network of human societies will also be integrated with the globally integrated system of the biosphere. We refer to this dawning age as the Akashic Age. As we mentioned in the introduction, the ancient rishis of India named the *Akasha* as a fifth element that is more fundamental than all the other four elements of the cosmos: fire, water, air, and earth. The *Akasha* is thus the fundamental dimension of the world—a dimension that is being rediscovered at the cutting edge of contemporary physics and cosmology—and which tells of our underlying universal connectivity.

The prospect that an Akashic Age would dawn for us is made plausible by the new scientific finding that we live in an interconnected, intrinsically nonlocal world. Everything that happens in one place can affect what happens in another place, and in some sense happens everywhere. This is the meaning of *nonlocality*. It is much more than the classical idea that one thing affects another, like one billiard ball hitting another ball and imparting its momentum to it. Classical cause and effect is limited by the classical limits of space and time—even electromagnetic waves attenuate in space and cease in time. True nonlocality is that one thing affects all other things, instantly and enduringly. Every single thing makes a lasting impression on the whole world. New findings in the sciences tell us that we are intrinsically interconnected—in the final analysis, we are one.

But the trend perceived in the systems sciences does not foretell what *will* happen, only what *could* happen—provided that there is no sharp break in the unfolding of the trend. Yet such a break is a distinct possibility: the evolution of social systems is subject to sudden and fundamental "bifurcations." Such cataclysmic breaks could appear in the form of globally destructive wars or a globally catastrophic degradation of the environment. If these bifurcations come about, there will not be any future at all—the planet will become uninhabitable. And even that would not contradict what we know about the unfolding of evolution: biological evolution brings some species on the scene, and dispatches others. Nearly 99 percent of all the biological species that have ever emerged on this planet have now become extinct; and a large proportion of the culturally specific human groups and societies that arose in human history have also vanished. Only the extent and the time scale of a future catastrophe would be new. Rather than involving one type of system, such as an organic species, an ecology, or a human sociocultural group, it would involve all of humanity and all of the biosphere, and it could last not for centuries but for millions of years.

If the basic evolutionary trends do not break down through a human-made or a natural catastrophe, the next step in the evolution of *Homo sapiens* will be the coming of an integrated, yet diversified, planetwide sociocultural system—the Akashic Age. This age will be characterized by a world civilization that is dynamic and complex, and organized on many levels, from the grass roots to the global. The fact that there is no certainty that the Akashic Age will come about should give us incentive to gather our wits and act. A sustainable global civilization *could* come about, and if it did, its advent would be in tune with the overall trend in the evolution of complex systems.

A positive unfolding of the evolutionary trend is entirely possible. But bringing it about depends on us—on what we do today, and in the next few years.

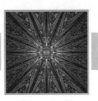

3

DILEMMAS AT THE
TURNING POINT

Modern humanity has been living in an intervening era between the last Ice Age and the present. In the general evolutionary run of things, this has been a very rapid, and short, ride. Over the past fifteen thousand years, humanity has engaged in an evolutionary process that has taken us from early hunter-gatherers to a stage of social development that is on the brink of forming a new evolutionary model—the Akashic Age of a conscious global species. During the last two centuries especially, we have witnessed an incredible wave of development. Through various cycles in the growth of civilizations (including numerous bifurcations of collapse and emergence), humanity has increased in social complexity. The complexity of our various global societies is such that we now find ourselves reaching the peak of this phase in our growth. We are approaching a new epoch: a planetary epoch.

THE PLANETARY EPOCH

By taking a brief glance at humanity's civilizing process, we can see that the shift from hunter-gatherers to farmers stemmed from a competition for resources, as farming yielded more energy than foraging. From this came the domestication of plants and animals, which archaeologists inform us appeared independently in various parts of the world between 11,000 and 5000 BCE.

Civilization building as we know it dates back to these original episodes of domestication that emerged after the end of the Ice Age (circa 11,000 to 5000 BCE). At that time, it appears that global warming created a geographical area whose conditions were better suited for humans to grow crops and gather together. The area in southwest Asia, around what are now known as the Tigris, Euphrates, and Jordan valleys—the so-called Fertile Crescent—saw the emergence of domesticated plants and animals. In turn, this high concentration of domesticated resources gave rise to the shift from foraging to farming. According to our known history, this area supported the first settled villages, perhaps earlier than 9000 BCE. Later, the earliest city-states in and around the region of Uruk, circa 3500 BCE, and subsequently at Sumer and Egypt, show some of the earliest known examples of what we would today call "energy-intensive" urban living.

This was followed by networks of cities that spread through Syria and the Levant, and through Iran, before finally springing up in Europe, notably along the southeastern coast of Spain. Yet, as some of these cities and states grew and developed, they ran into the same pattern of resource problems. The solution was to transform themselves into empires. This is the now-familiar pattern throughout the social evolution of our species. Crudely put, the pattern looks like this:

Larger population growth → More complex lifestyles → Greater need for resources → Increased military buildup → Empire building → Colonization by force or underhanded coercion

This underlying pattern has characterized our species as we passed from hunter-gatherer and agrarian cultures, to city-states, industrialized society, and now as we stand on the brink of a planetary stage of development. Cultural historian William Irwin Thompson has marked these eras:

1   Hominization: 4,000,000–200,000 BCE
2   Symbolization: 200,000–10,000 BCE
3   Agriculturalization: 10,000–3,500 BCE

4 Civilization: 3,500 BCE–1500 CE

5 Industrialization: 1500–1945 CE

6 Planetization: 1945–present[1]

The end result of this post–Ice Age phase is a population of seven billion on planet Earth. Added to this are vast interconnected (yet highly unequal) networks that feed the flow of energy, resources, materials, finance, information, and communications. Indeed, if we take just a brief glance at some of the features of our current globalized world, we might be mistaken for thinking we already inhabit a planetary society.

- Communications: With the Internet and global communication systems, we have an "always-on" flow of news and information.
- Language: Several languages are manifesting as global, such as English, Chinese, and Spanish; this is encouraged by our global communication systems.
- Economy: We are seeing the emergence of global economic markets, financial trade agreements, economic blocs, economics beyond nation-states.
- Culture: Cultural trends are dispersed globally—films, music, food, fashion, sports, etc.
- Environment: Threats and consequences are now global, with domino effects being felt worldwide.
- Travel: Global mobility and tourism now allow for worldwide forms of contact, exposure, and shared experiences
- Boundaries: We are witnessing a weakening of the nation-state and a blurring of frontiers, plus widespread migration from one place to another, and larger international political blocs—EU (European Union), AU (African Union), UNASUR (Union of South American Nations), AL (Arab League), and ASEAN (Association of Southeast Asian Nations).
- Work: People live and work in different regions/countries; they often work from home or engage in online commerce; many live as migrant workers.

Our great planetary web of interrelations and interconnections is the result of some thirteen thousand years of social development, following a familiar pattern relating to the capture, storage, and usage of available energies. In the 1940s, anthropologist Leslie White proposed a single equation for all human history:

$$E \times T \to C \; ; \text{where } E = \text{energy}; T = \text{technology}; \text{and } C = \text{culture}$$

Because of this need to efficiently utilize available energies, humans have gone on a rampage in capturing and organizing ever more energy in their rapid development from village, to city, to nations, and finally to empire building. Some of these empires had to transform themselves into industrial economies in order to maintain the $E \times T \to C$ equation. The resulting human cultures (C) had to consistently evolve more intricate social structures, or they imploded if/when they exceeded the long-term carrying capacity of their environment.

For example, many well-known agricultural empires in the past hit a ceiling of development and collapsed because they were not able to locate the next wave of energy resources to rise beyond these limits. The only way to surpass such resource limits is to shift into a more energy-intensive mode, which was exactly what happened in the West when fossil-fuel energy was discovered. Since that energetic leap, social development has been on a wild ride. According to Ian Morris, author of *Why the West Rules—For Now:*

> In the fourteen thousand years between the end of the Ice Age and 2000 CE, social development rose nine hundred points [according to author's own scale of measurement]. In the next hundred years [according to trends] it will rise *four thousand points more*. Nine hundred points took us from the cave paintings of Altamira to the atomic age; where will another four thousand take us?[2]

According to Morris's own calculations, between 2000 and 2050, social development will rise twice as much as in the previous fifteen thousand years. Can we imagine what this means for the definition of human life? We are approaching what Morris terms the "greatest discontinuity in history." That's only the good side of the news, however.

There is also a flip side: we may never make it to this level of global social development. We could very likely reach a new "hard ceiling" of resource/energy availability, which would first stall growth, then lead to implosion. The Roman Empire ran up against a similar hard ceiling in the first century CE, which led to its collapse, followed by a six-century decline that dragged Europe into the Dark Ages.

The current prognosis does not look good. According to current trends, world population is set to increase to 9 billion by 2050, which would place increasing pressure onto already fragile, some say depleting, energy resources. The International Energy Agency expects world demand for oil to rise to 116 million barrels per day by 2030, and even then the agency estimates that 1.4 billion people will be without electricity. Are we arriving at what some are calling the end of growth? Is our current global project at its peak, the crest of the wave, and now set for a catastrophic bifurcation, a downward spiral into contraction, localization, and breakup?

Life in the second decade of the twenty-first century is poised to enter new territory—on the verge of major local and global discontinuity. On almost a daily basis, we are now reading headlines about extreme weather, from severe droughts and flooding to increased earthquake activity and devastating hurricanes, tornadoes, tsunamis, and cyclones. On top of this, we hear about impending resource depletion, spiraling food costs, financial collapse, national sovereign debt crises, regional instability and military intervention, domestic security incidents, and the list goes on.

It is not surprising, then, that many people sense that things are getting out of control and that our societies are facing critical times. What this amounts to is that our current social-global systems are stressed to the max already. A major crisis—being hit by multiple shocks simultaneously—would produce a critical instability: a systemwide bifurcation.

Our old models are—in two words—stressed out, and in need of replacement. That is why we foresee the coming years consisting of a series of system shocks that are set to lead up to a decisive bifurcation that will mark where the old models fall and the new models emerge in their stead. Of course, there is also the possibility that the old models will implode, leaving a space to be filled.

THE COMING BIFURCATION

Because of the rapid growth of economic and sociocultural globalization in recent decades, humanity now faces a range of disturbances and shocks that will have a worldwide impact. Some of these system shocks will be caused by a bottleneck when various systems are unable to maintain their stability. That is, if they pass the threshold of their stability (when the bottleneck gets too tight), there will be increased discontinuity until, if not righted, things will fall apart. If this happens, a bifurcation will occur—perhaps rapidly. Yet such a process is not always outwardly visible or obvious at first. This is because the overall structure remains in place, even as the internal dynamics begin to come apart. We continue to look at the façade of the building while, from the inside, the bailiffs have removed all the furniture. If too many internal connections begin to fail (come apart) at once, this then affects the larger pattern of the structural dynamics, and it becomes obvious to all at the last minute. Thus the bifurcation is the result of too many instabilities and shocks that the system is no longer able to absorb.

Such instabilities are already occurring in the following areas of the global system: financial structures (bankruptcies and corruption), politics (corruption and ineptitude), deficient or missing welfare support and health care, social cohesion, and food (increasing prices and scarcity), to name just a few. Shocks within these core systems, so essential to our everyday lives, will have a ricochet effect within the psyche of many people worldwide. This, in turn, will lead to displays of public anger, strikes in response to austerity measures, protests against financial irregularities, anger at military interventions and saber rattling, and hostility against the insecurity of living within an unpredictable and unstable environment.

Within this period of rapid system shocks we are likely to witness a shift in values and priorities. One of these could be a switch in perceived value between so-called "notional" wealth and "real" wealth. That is, the value of our financial transactions ("notional" wealth) will decline as the value of real-world skills and knowledge ("real" wealth) increases. If this occurs, it will signal a wealth transfer from "paper debt" to "people capacity." This shift, together with its social repercussions, may also prompt a shift in values, such as life priorities, social goals, and so forth.

The bifurcation we are now approaching as we reach the cusp of a planetary era could spark a global awakening. A wave of awakening may open people's eyes to the dysfunctional state of our current systems. The coming system shocks could create a great wave of creativity, which would last for years, perhaps decades, if circumstances continued to create the necessity for social change. Such social creativity could set in motion a transition away from top-down structures (vertical) and toward the rise of collaborative, self-organized, and distributed networks (horizontal). That is, a shift from authoritarian hierarchical structures to democratic, participatory networks. As we explore later in the book, we are likely to see more and more creative and frustrated people abandoning current dysfunctional systems in order to take the future into their own hands. Responses to system breakdowns will be increasingly "outside the box"— unexpected and unpredictable—and yet based on collaboration, connectivity, and consciousness. Sometimes a shock is exactly what is needed to awaken the sleeper.

It would be a great shame if our present cultural evolutionary project—which took humanity from foragers to the cusp of a planetary era—were to collapse just before it managed to shift into the Akashic Age. The bottom line, it seems, is that we need to undergo a revolution in our resource systems in order to break through the hard ceiling that stands in the way of further growth. Just as oil superseded coal, we need new sources of energy as well as new models of global efficiency and social restructuring to come to the fore. If our resource systems could be remodeled, our energy-matter relations redefined, we could just make that leap into an unprecedented era of social transformation that would make the Industrial Revolution look like a toddler's early steps.

We are now at the critical stage in which we need to make a shift— from attempting to sustain our intrinsically unsustainable society to taking concerted action aimed at transforming it. That is why the next decade may well be the most important in the history of humanity.

CRITICAL THRESHOLDS ON ARRIVING
AT THE PLANETARY EPOCH

It is no understatement to say that humanity has arrived at the planetary epoch that dawns at the twenty-first century amid revolutions in energy and communications that have transformed sociocultural life, predominantly in the developed Western nations. The whole world has now been brought closer together. Pathways of interrelations and interdependencies have grown far and wide—trade, culture, language, entertainment, travel, leisure activities, and even war and terrorism—and are now the common threads that tie us into an international embrace of global civilization and citizenry. However, that global embrace has been costly, and mostly paid for on the back of a relatively cheap, and once-plentiful source of energy. It now seems that our present civilization has all but wasted it in a century and a half of extreme extravagance. In terms of the bigger picture, the future may be divided, and defined, between those regions that will be resource sources (exporting energy) and those that become resource sinks (importing energy). In going global, we have entered—and entertained—a new myth: infinite growth within a world of finite resources.

The situation now staring us all directly in the face is that our environmental and social systems have entered a phase of heightened stress. The future cannot unfold along the current trends; the narrative of our time—perpetual growth—is simply not feasible. This is not a matter of speculation, but rather a law of physics.

As a civilization, we are in the throes of a historical bifurcation: living out an endgame. Not the endgame of our species, however, but the endgame of an epoch. For many of us living in the developed nations, we are witnessing the endgame of the Second Industrial Revolution. Yet, overall, this endgame concerns a way of living, a sociopolitical model that has now come to the end of its tenure. Simply put, we cannot go on living as we have been doing for the past 150 years—since oil was first discovered and utilized for fueling our rapid social expansion.

The basis for all life is a living system, and this system requires the continual inflow of energy/information in order not to atrophy. This is the law of entropy. At regular stages of growth, new energy inputs are required in order to boost the growth and expansion of the system. For millennia, the human species has been evolving toward a planetary epoch. We are now on the cusp of this evolutionary stage, and the reason we managed to arrive at this point so rapidly is due to fossil-fueled economic growth that enabled the human population to expand dramatically, leading to an explosion in research, development, and activity on an ever-widening scale. The myth of perpetual growth (which, for many, is still a reality) requires more manufacturing, more trade, and more consumerism to feed it. This, in turn, all requires more energy. And not just any form of energy, but sources of energy that are concentrated, controllable, and have the greatest returns. From these sources we have been able to construct sophisticated infrastructures that circumnavigate the globe, oil-fertilize our agriculture into mass food production, illuminate our rooms instantly, fly us to other countries as if taking a taxi, and create access to a kaleidoscope of goods and services one could only have dreamed of previously.

All this because we could tap into the most precious energy source so far discovered on the planet. Our current 150 years of rapid industrial acceleration has been built on the notion of a perpetual-growth machine. This extraordinary period in our cultural evolution has now been accepted, and taught, as the norm. Yet back in the early 1970s, the Club of Rome's Limits to Growth report concluded that the end of growth would probably arrive between 2010 and 2050. This realization, and its consequences, is soon to hit home.

Let us be realistic: from now on, only relative growth is possible. Some aspects of the global economy may continue to grow relative to others, yet the overall trend will be one of contraction. Those who support continued growth often forget that there are factors external to the economic system that in the coming years will make business as usual all but impossible. Further, this situation is not temporary but permanent. These factors include the depletion of important resources, the proliferation of disruptive environmental impacts, and a financial system that is no longer suited to the current crisis. However, there is another significant factor that most futurists fail to take into account, perhaps because it cannot be physically verified—the presence of human consciousness. That is, a shift in the pervading consciousness of any given era can—and indeed does—have dramatic consequences. This is especially so in the sphere of social action, as we highlight throughout this book. But for now our focus is on the critical thresholds that are likely to play out in the years ahead, or are already in play as we speak.

As we have noted, arriving at the twenty-first century, at the cusp of a planetary civilization, has had many costs. Until now we have been paying those costs through a generous gift of nature that we have taken too much for granted, and that is now about to run out. Our expanding global societies, with their increasing levels of complexity, exact a higher resource cost to maintain than simpler ones. When available resources begin to fail to meet those rising costs, we can no longer expect our increasing returns to come in. Unless a new source of energy, equivalent or better, replaces the existing one, society is likely to fragment. In the past this has been used as a euphemism for *collapse*.[3] When this has occurred in the past, it has been accompanied by declining population levels, social disruption and hardship, a loss of centralized governing power, and a shift in cultural-political arrangements. This has been because of two overriding factors: (1) there was limited, or no, collapse preparedness, meaning that there was nothing set up to prepare the society and its people for a period of failing systems; and (2) past societies did not possess the level, or type, of technologies needed to put in place a new model that could continue to support social, resource, political, and, in our case, global, sustainability.

Our view is that because of the bifurcation likely to come about in the next phase of our social evolution, our current unstable systems will begin to break down and fall away. Other systems will arise to fill the gaps. There are already signs that there is a building up of collapse preparedness within individuals, communities, and organizations, as well as credible evidence that a shift toward a decentralized, distributed, and collaborative model is not only possible but is now under way.

First, however, we need to get a fuller picture of our situation by taking a brief look at some of the critical thresholds affecting human society in the second decade of the twenty-first century.

Depleting Resources

There has already been much written on the subject of our depleting global resources (see the bibliography and recommended reading section), so our intention here is to briefly sketch the scenario that will unfold in the coming years. Also, it is important to recognize that the resource situation is intricately linked to our global economic situation. That is, when we have a disturbance on the global economic scene, this affects our worldwide resource infrastructure—from the supply and demand costs to transport and delivery, and the ability of the wholesale market to absorb rising costs. Similarly, a glitch in resource availability, procurement, costs, and the like directly affects the fragile nature of our interlinked economies. This is part of the reason why the decade ahead is so critical—because our dire global economic system has a domino effect on a whole range of interlinked systems.

The social and geopolitical ramifications are huge, and we are already seeing this in sovereign-state instability, major bankruptcies, austerity measures, and social protest becoming regular features of daily life. Ideally, we would need to see worldwide energy prices decrease dramatically in order to avoid an increasingly constrained global economy. However, this seems unlikely as global demand is on the increase (especially from China and India), geopolitical tensions are escalating (Iran and the Middle East), and our economies are teetering on the brink of collapse. Also, for the foreseeable future, any new sources of energy that are on the scene are likely to have lower net energy capacity than conventional fossil fuels have had historically: fossil fuels give out much energy for relatively little input. Human civilization, on the whole, has become energy-intensive, and the renewable energies that are poised to replace fossil fuels are not nearly as energy-intensive.

Of particular importance here is not only the nature of the energy sources, but how they are utilized within energy-intensive systems that are themselves composed of a vast array of interconnected material systems and structures. In complex systems, energy storage and use is just as crucial as energy capture. It is not only a question of energy itself, but a matter of the material structures that store and distribute energy locally and globally. Thus, as we explore in the book, the immediate future is likely to be based on an increasingly distributed model—in energy, communications, and connections—rather than the intensive, centralized model that has been in place for at least the last 150 years. It is this intensive, centralized model that reshaped food production in the Western world. Fossil fuels (used in fertilizers, pesticides, farm machinery, packaging, distribution, etc.) were able to create a production model whereby just 2 percent of the population became the growers of nearly all our domestically produced food in the Western Hemisphere. The other 98 percent are now narrowly trained to focus on other matters, leaving knowledge about and skill in cultivating the land in desperately few hands.

The situation rapidly emerging in the twenty-first century is that global food demand is gradually outstripping our systems of supply. As Richard Heinberg notes:

> Food producers' ability to meet growing needs is increasingly being strained by rising human populations, falling freshwater supplies, the rise of biofuels industries, expanding markets within industrializing nations for more resource-intensive meat- and fish-based diets; dwindling wild fisheries; and climate instability. The result will almost inevitably be a worldwide food crisis sometime in the next two or three decades.[4]

Added to this list we have the recent, and ongoing, environmental disruptions that are wreaking havoc on our crop harvests. A recent example was the severe drought in Russia (in late 2010), which destroyed around a third of its wheat crop. As a result, Russia declared a ban on all wheat exports, sending up the price of food worldwide. There were hikes in bread prices in various countries, which led to local food riots, such as the deadly ones in Mozambique. Following this, the UN's Food and Agricultural Organization held a special meeting in Rome to discuss the issue of food security. Julian Cribb, scientist and author of *The Coming Famine,* has stated that "The most urgent issue confronting humanity in the next 50 years is not climate change or the financial crisis, it is whether we can achieve and sustain such a harvest [our global food systems]."[5] In recent years there have been notable increases worldwide in the prices of wheat, cocoa, coffee, sugar, and meat. And for the first time in modern history, China became a net importer of corn, largely used for animal feed. Experts believe that increasing food prices will lead to further civil unrest and rioting, especially in developing countries.

Signs of this social unrest have already emerged, as seen in the dramatic explosion of protests and rioting at the start of 2011 in what became known as the Arab Spring. While some of this was sparked by corrupt regimes, it also stemmed from public anger over escalating food costs, as staple commodities were hit hard by inflation. Continued climatic disruptions affecting food production in North America, Europe, and Asia have exacerbated this situation.

In the coming years we are likely to witness a great deal more public anger on the streets as social austerity, financial woes, and increasing food and energy prices literally ignite a cauldron of dissent and frustration. Many people, who in the past might have had no reason to protest, might suddenly find themselves the new victims of social, political, and economic exclusion. The consequences of social alienation could lead to civil unrest and socially disruptive behavior. A recent example of this was the sporadic riots that erupted first in London, and then spread to other U.K. cities, in August 2011. One security expert has recently concluded that we are in for a "great reckoning," a "new twenty years' crisis," and a "long hot century."[6]

Another major area of concern, which will soon become more prominent on the world stage, is water access. As the global demand for food production increases, so will the need for increased water supplies. To date, agricultural farming accounts for 66 percent of the world's water use; this does not include industrial and personal/household use. It has been calculated that by 2025 over half the world's population will live in places that are subject to severe water stress, and that "the world will nearly have run out of existing water supplies by the mid twenty-first century."[7] Currently, it is estimated that many of the world's major "food bowls" [agricultural food producing regions] are suffering from lack of regular water as environmental patterns shift. Just as in the case of fossil fuels, water will become a disputed resource, triggering so-called energy wars in the very near future, with various nation-states arguing over how much disputed and/or shared water sources belong to their territory. In fact, there have already been instances of nations attempting to redirect water sources. For example, in 2006 Uganda cut the flow of water out of Lake Victoria into the River Nile.

Another major issue is that there is a significant discrepancy between available freshwater (runoff) and population. For example, Asia has 36 percent of runoff but 60 percent of the world's people. By contrast, South America has 26 percent of runoff but only 6 percent of the population. In areas where there are large, urban populations, we will likely see increased instances of water being redirected from agricultural land/food production to supplying urban cities; such is the case in China. As urban growth increases, the issue of food and water supplies will become more urgent.

Electricity production requires water as well. It is calculated that, for example, about 49 percent of the 410 billion gallons of water the United States withdraws daily goes to cooling thermoelectric and coal-burning power plants.[8] If the nuclear lobby continues to support expansion in the future, substantially more water will be required to cool nuclear reactors.

Desalination, too, will prove to be important in the years ahead for nations that have little or no freshwater. Saudi Arabia alone accounts for 20 percent of global desalination; the problem here is that this requires huge amounts of energy. While Saudi Arabia now has oil to use as energy for desalination projects, this is liable to change in the future, when Middle Eastern nations will find themselves facing increasing shortfalls of available clean water.

An issue less in the public eye concerns the declining availability of metals, especially rare earth elements (REEs), of which there are seventeen. These metals, as their name implies, are found in relatively small quantities. Their uses, however, are wide and varied; for example, in superconductors, factory tools and agricultural machinery, the infrastructure of highways, pipes, power lines, radar, fiber-optic communications, televisions, computers, mobile phones, and various sensitive military applications. China currently produces over 97 percent of the world's supply of rare earth metals, and in late 2009 announced plans to extensively cut its export quota over the coming years in order to conserve domestic supply.

There have also been troubling signs that recent clashes, such as Japan's dispute with China over maritime boundaries, have led China to temporarily cut off supplies of rare earth metals. Such metals are highly sought after and are essential for an array of critical systems, including energy production. All these metals are currently being depleted, and some are already at worrying levels of scarcity.

The issue of depleted global resources is not mere speculation. The current state of the world shows that a struggle for resources is clearly under way. However, it is dictated by a strategy of conquest and competition, rather than collaboration and sharing. Recent institutional reports, such as those by Lloyds of London and the World Economic Forum, recognize that a short-term energy crunch is likely and could have serious social and political consequences.

The depletion of nonrenewable energy resources is critical in how our complex global civilization is able to sustain its internal interdependencies, interlinking systems, and material infrastructures. We foresee new models being developed based on community networks, and more local values. Part of this transformation will be brought about by economic instabilities in the global marketplace.

Financial Crisis

If this hasn't played out already, then the years from now until 2020 will see a continuation of the systemic crisis that brought about the global financial crisis (also referred to as the Great Recession) of 2008. The global financial system is intrinsically unsustainable with its labyrinthine financial agreements. These include mortgage-backed securities, collateralized debt obligations, credit default swaps, predatory lending, derivatives, off-balance-sheet financing, and the like. The financial system has become an almost impossible marketplace to regulate, as risky mortgages and debts are funded through what is known as the "shadow banking system," which is further obscured from external checks and balances.

As already noted, the current myth of a perpetual growth economy requires a relatively cheap and plentiful supply of resources, together with expanding markets. With energy and resource constraints affecting the global marketplace at a critical time of great economic instability, the result is a time bomb waiting to explode.

The global effects of the ongoing Great Recession are felt through the actions of giant financial institutions, as well as by the policies of sovereign nations that are riddled with debt, such as Greece, Spain, Portugal, and other Mediterranean countries within the European Union. Losses worldwide to date have been in the trillions (whether in dollars, pounds, or euros), and the ongoing rounds of quantitative easing and bailouts only serve to further bewilder, frustrate, and anger the people. For many, *bailout fatigue* is now an all-too-familiar phrase, signaling that the ineffective actions being taken by governments are increasingly remote from more and more people's sense of reality. We expect that the years ahead, from now until 2020, will be marked by additional economic disruptions, increasing bankruptcies and bank failures, and further pressure on many nation-states to implement highly unpopular austerity measures.

Governments are likely to become more repressive in the face of financial instability and mounting debt. This will almost certainly result in a curtailing of freedom of expression and civil rights as social protests grow. This is the danger of a social model predicated on the expectation of continued growth. We have to face the prospect of a future in which our once-cheap consumer lifestyles are no longer cheap. This will indeed be the case when resource and economic growth falters in countries like China.

A radical overhaul of the global economy is not only necessary, it is inevitable. Where this leads to in terms of currency markets is uncertain. It may be that in the short term a major simplification of the economy will be the immediate reaction to the global contraction of economic growth. This is even more likely when we take into account the economic fallout from increasingly disruptive environmental impacts and the related costs.

Disruptive Environmental Impacts

Although the world has always experienced natural disasters and accidents in the past, the world of today is significantly different. Because of exponential population growth, we have transformed our species into urban dwellers. The twenty-first century has become the century of urbanization. In the late 1990s, the world's population was growing by about 900 million per decade, the largest absolute increases in human history.[9] This is equivalent to a new London every month. At this rate, world population is expected to reach over 9 billion by 2050. More than half the world's population now lives in urban areas, with the UN forecasting that 60 percent of the global population will live in cities by 2030. It appears that we now inhabit an "urban planet."

Modern cities are the largest structures ever created. Tokyo, for example, has around 13 million residents (35 million in the Greater Tokyo Area). São Paulo is estimated to have approximately 11 million residents (unofficial estimates place the population at 23 million). These megacities will soon be joined by others in the developing world, such as Mumbai, Delhi, Mexico City, Dhaka, Jakarta, and Lagos. These will be accompanied by rapid growth in the number of cities between 5 million and 10 million, as well as by cities with populations between 1 million and 5 million. By 2015 it is estimated that there will be twenty-three megacities (nineteen of them in the developing world) and thirty-seven cities with populations between 5 million and 10 million.[10]

Much of the population flow into cities comes from refugees. In 1978 there were fewer than 6 million refugees; by 2005 there were 21 million, and by 2006, 32.9 million. The UN refugee agency's Global Trends 2010 report states that, worldwide, 43.7 million people were forcibly displaced by conflict and environmental disruption by the end of 2010. These numbers are likely to rise further as climatic changes and global conflict continue to displace large communities in mainly rural and poorer parts of the world. Yet it is not only in developing countries where natural disasters and accidents are wreaking havoc. Recent examples include:

- The earthquake in Haiti in 2010, which left 310,000 people dead, 300,000 injured, 1 million homeless, and virtually destroyed the island's economy.
- The 2010 earthquake in Chile, where 9 percent of the population lost their homes and losses to the economy of Chile were estimated at $15–30 billion.

- The BP Deepwater Horizon oil rig explosion in the Gulf of Mexico in 2010, the largest accidental marine oil spill in the history of the petroleum industry. The spill caused extensive damage to marine and wildlife habitat, fisheries, tourism, wetlands, and shorelines, and allegedly people's health. The Gulf seas may take decades to fully recover from the contamination.

- Floods in Pakistan in 2010 that submerged a fifth of the country and directly affected about 20 million people, mostly by destruction of property, livelihood, and infrastructure. Total economic impact has been estimated at $43 billion.

- Russian wildfires that destroyed millions of acres of crops and subsequent grain harvests. The fires caused roughly $15 billion in damages.

Natural disasters are exacting an increasingly high toll that is directly impacting nation-states' ability to absorb the damage, both financially and in terms of critical infrastructure. As resource needs become ever more critical, riskier extraction methods are likely to cause worse environmental impacts and accidents. Rising environmental costs tend to accumulate until a crisis occurs and systems collapse. Our rapid pace of urbanization, the interdependency of our infrastructures, and the industrialization of our food systems has created a model that is increasingly vulnerable to environmental disruptions.

The Coming Bottleneck

It is now clear that many of the systems we have come to rely on are in a state of critical vulnerability. The coming decade will involve a series of unpredictable risks that are economic, environmental, geopolitical, societal, and technological. As nation-states contend with the old model of conquest and competition to sustain economic growth, there will be an escalation in the struggle for control of resources that will shift geopolitical relations throughout the world. We should not underestimate the covert maneuvering set to take place on the world stage during the next decade. Already, such nations as China and Saudi Arabia are buying farmland in Australia, New Zealand, and South America. North and South America, Europe, Asia, and the Middle East are all hot spots where aspects of this "great game" will be played out. The Middle East, for example, has vast oil wealth, yet it is beset by extreme economic inequality, political corruption and instability, and the need to import critical resources, such as food and water. The Arab Spring protests, as we have already mentioned, were warning shots, telling the world that the people will no longer tolerate these situations. What erupted surprised almost everybody and further major destabilizations are more than likely. Our predominant urban lifestyles, enmeshed within infrastructures that many of us are dependent upon (such as our daily supply chains), may soon become enormous liabilities as our current models prove too slow to adapt to changing needs.

In the short term we may find that the political response is to try to arrange the world into more regionalized and hierarchical structures, driven by fears over national and regional security. Conditions may become unstable for a while as the world passes through a bottleneck of oil, food, and water resource depletion; financial breakdown and reordering; disruptive environmental impacts; and social backlash. As we move into a period where our global systems lack the energy inflow needed to sustain and maintain their complex material infrastructures, we may be compelled to invest once again in our communities and local economic networks. In addition to economic restructuring, we will also need to rethink our transport systems, energy networks, and food production and distribution systems. We are heading into a decade where we will literally have to rearrange the way we live.

A TIME TO SHIFT

Even to a casual observer, it would appear that our behavior is utterly inappropriate and out of step when it comes to dealing with the challenges we now face. Our inadequate individual and collective preparedness falls far short of our sociocultural and technological evolution. When there is a rapidly deteriorating mix of natural and human systems, driven by an irrational belief system, such as the myth of perpetual growth, sooner rather than later the global juggernaut will plunge off a cliff. Either we recognize the unsustainability of our predicament and adapt our ways to create new social, political, economic, environmental, and cultural systems that will usher in the Akashic Age—or else we will find ourselves struggling to come to terms with a planet that no longer fosters our human welfare.

In the coming years, we will inevitably incur sudden bifurcations, as we can no longer avert some significant tipping points. These bifurcations, however, will act as the catalysts to spur humanity into accelerated change. All of us on the planet are faced with the necessity of reevaluating how we coordinate social, economic, and environmental concerns and interdependencies. Shifting to a new model—of interconnectivity and collective empathy—is now fundamentally a question of when and how—not if. We must take action to bring about a future that benefits the majority in a sustainable and equitable way. The writing has been on the wall for a long time now. Vested interests (although dedicated to amassing their own wealth and power) have kept the wolf from our doors—until now. While some people may have the means to hunker down and ride out the coming shocks, the rest of us do not have this luxury. Nor should we, for it is a sugarcoated luxury that blinds us to a momentous opportunity for real and lasting change. These changes have not only structural but, more important, behavioral implications.

As we shall discuss at greater length later, the needed new thinking and action are likely to be generated not by the current centralized, top-down systems but by more democratic, decentralized, and bottom-up systems. Oriented by timely and functional values and beliefs, these systems have the potential to create networks of cooperation, collaboration, and creativity in and through grassroots communities. We believe that the rise of these new collaborative networks will usher in the Akashic Age.

PART TWO

At the Threshold of the Akashic Age

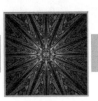

4

SHIFTING OUR VALUES
AND BELIEFS

The new thinking we need will not emerge all at once, in one fell swoop. It will come about—and is already coming about—as contemporary thinking is increasingly questioned. There is a step before we can embrace new ideas: it is to put the old on trial.

Human thinking, aside from the rigorous branches of science and philosophy, is dominated by values and beliefs—some conscious, others not. Those that guide our thinking today need to be made conscious, so we could question them, put them on trial. Are they ethical? Are they reasonable? Do they serve our lives and the life of all the people who populate this planet? Do they inspire actions and behavior that enable seven billion people to live in peace, in reasonable well-being, and with a reasonable level of sustainability?

As we shall see, in regard to some of our most widespread values and beliefs, this is not the case.

SIX NOXIOUS PERSONAL BELIEFS

1. I am what I am—an individual making my way in an uncaring, indifferent, and often hostile world. I am responsible only for ensuring my own interests.
2. I owe allegiance only to one country, and the government is required to look after my own interests.

3. The value of everything, including human beings, can be calculated in terms of money. What every economy needs is growth, and what every person wants is to get rich.

4. Newer is always better. It is desirable, and for the economy even necessary, to buy and use the latest products and technologies. They make our economy grow and then everybody is better off.

5. The world will run the way it has always been running; crisis is a temporary disturbance after which business will again operate as usual.

6. The long-term future is none of my business. Why should I worry about the next generation? Every generation, like every person, has to look after itself.

FIVE LETHAL CULTURAL BELIEFS

Some outdated beliefs are shared by entire communities and cultures. They need to be examined in greater detail.

1. The Neolithic Illusion: Nature Is Inexhaustible

The belief that nature is a limitless resource and provides an infinite sink for waste goes back thousands of years. Originally, the historic belief in the inexhaustibility of nature was understandable and innocuous. Human tribes and groups did not overstep the limits of nature's capacity to regenerate the required resources; they lived in balance with their environment. This changed with the advent of the Neolithic Age, about 10,000 years ago. In the Fertile Crescent, now the Middle East, people were not content to live within the rhythms and cycles of nature, but sought ways to harness the forces of their environment. In some places, such as ancient Sumer, human practices had vexing consequences. In deforested lands, flash floods washed away irrigation channels and dams, and left fields arid. In the course of millennia of cultivation, the Fertile Crescent of biblical times became an arid region, dominated by sandy desert. But it did not occur to the people of ancient Babylon, Sumer, Egypt, India, and China that their environment could ever cease to supply them with edible plants, domestic animals, clean water, and breathable air, or be fouled by waste and garbage. Nature seemed far too vast to be tainted, polluted, or defiled by human activity. The insight that we live on a small planet—one with finite resources—that we can taint, pollute, and defile by the intended or unintended by-products of our activities—did not dawn on most people until Rachel Carson published her pathbreaking book *Silent Spring* in 1962.

Persisting in the Neolithic Illusion would be lethal. It would lead to the overuse of vital resources and the overload of nature's self-regenerative cycles. In early times this was not an insuperable problem, for people could move on, colonizing new lands and exploiting fresh resources. But in the planetary epoch of the twenty-first century, when we overexploit and destroy one environment after another, we have nowhere left to go. Ever more people will have to do with an ever-scarcer supply of irreplaceable natural resources.

The overuse of natural resources is impacting the health and the very survival of more and more people. We are already witnessing more and more increasingly severe natural disasters. This is a problem because the resilience of our ecosystems is impaired by human activity. Even more dramatically, in a matter of a few years there may not be sufficient resources to feed all the people in the world. There are 3 billion malnourished people today, and when population peaks at around 9 billion, this figure could easily double.

2. Social Darwinism: The Ideology of Competitive Fitness

Another age-old belief, the idea that competition is the basis of all life, was given fresh impetus by Darwin's theory of evolution through natural selection. In classical Darwinism, the entire evolution of life from unicellular organisms to higher primates is determined by genetic mutation guided by natural selection. The principal mechanism of evolution is the survival of the fittest and the militant strategy of the selfish gene. The social application of this theory, known as Social Darwinism, holds that in society, as in nature, a process of competitive selection eliminates the unfit; that is, only the fit survive. This is taken to mean that if we want to survive, we have to be fit for the struggle for life—fitter than our competitors. In this context, fitness is not determined by our genes. It is a personal and cultural trait, such as shrewdness, daring, ambition, and the ability to acquire money and put it to work.

In the 1930s and early 1940s, Social Darwinism was an inspiration of the Nazi ideology. It justified the conquest of foreign territories in the name of creating *Lebensraum* (living space) for Germany, and was put forward as a justification for the genocide of Jews, Slavs, and Gypsies. The fitness—defined as the racial purity—of the Aryan race was to be preserved at all costs. In our day, Social Darwinism has not disappeared, although it is not as virulent as in Nazi Germany. Armed might is still used to secure perceived interests, whether they are territorial or economic.

In today's world, the struggle for survival also emerges in the subtler but equally merciless struggle of competitors in business. In this struggle, fitness rewards corporate executives, international financiers, and speculators: they become rich and powerful. The resulting gap between rich and poor creates frustration and leads to violence, but the "fit" can largely ignore these consequences. The economic variant of Social Darwinism is as lethal as its military variant.

3. Market Fundamentalism:
Whatever the Question, the Market Is the Answer

In the industrialized world, mainstream business and political leaders elevate the market to the status of a tribal god. They accept pollution and climate change as the unavoidable costs of competition on the market; they sacrifice to it farmlands, forests, wetlands and prairies, ecosystems and watersheds. They justify their stance by maintaining that the market distributes the benefits, so if my company or my country's economy does well, other companies and countries will also do well.

The "ideology of the market"—which, in practice becomes the *idolatry* of the market—rests on a handful of fundamental beliefs.

- All human needs and wants can be expressed in monetary terms and can enter the market as a form of demand with corresponding supply. Satisfying demand fuels the economy and is good for everybody.

- Satisfying needs and wants has no absolute limits. There are no insuperable human, financial, or natural limits to the conversion of needs and wants into salable commodities.
- Competition on the open market is both necessary and good: it is the governing principle of all economic and social relations.
- The freedom to compete on the market is the basis of human liberty and the foundation of social and economic justice.

These are the tenets of market fundamentalism, and they are wrong. They fail to take into account, first, that we live on a small planet with finite human and natural resources and a finite capacity to absorb the waste and pollution that accompanies most forms of industrial production, and, second, that competition in the market favors the rich at the expense of the poor.

Everybody knows the adverse effects of waste and pollution; we see them on the climate; on the quality of air, water, and land; and on the regenerative capacity of crops, pastures, fishing grounds, and forests. Economists, in turn, know that the market distributes benefits only under conditions of near-perfect competition, where the playing field is level and all players have more or less the same number of chips. It is evident that in today's world the field is far from level and the chips are far from evenly distributed. Even entering the market requires money, and with few, if notable, exceptions, money in the form of credit is accessible only to those who already have money, or can offer substantial collateral.

Market fundamentalism is a lethal cultural belief. Our finite planet sets limits on indiscriminate forms of economic growth, and the current market economy is racing toward those limits. The rich, though fewer in number, are still becoming richer, and the tidal waves of poverty keep rising. The economic and social system of the world is becoming dangerously unbalanced.

4. Consumerism: The More You Have, the Better You Are

This typically modern belief justifies the struggle for profit and wealth. It posits a direct relationship between the size of our wallet, as demonstrated by our ability to acquire material possessions, and our personal worth as the owner of the wallet and possessor of the goods money can buy.

In the past, the equation of human worth with the possession of and consumption of material goods was consciously fueled by business; companies advertised conspicuous consumption as the ideal lifestyle. But consumerism is another lethal cultural belief. It leads to overconsumption and resource depletion, and is neither healthy nor sustainable. The hoarding of material possessions by an individual, like the single-minded pursuit of natural and financial resources by a country, is a sign of insecurity, not intelligence.

5. Militarism: The Way to Peace Is through War

The ancient Romans had a saying: If you aspire to peace, prepare for war. This matched their conditions and experience. The Romans had a world-wide empire, with rebellious peoples and cultures within and barbarian tribes at the periphery. Maintaining this empire required a constant exercise of military power. Today the nature of power is very different, but the belief about war is much the same. Like Rome in classical times, the United States is a global power, but one that is economic rather than political. Maintaining that position of global strength requires not armed enforcement but fair and sustainable relations between the nations of the world, and the entire human system and its life-supporting ecology.

War is not the way to achieve peace and sustainability. Instead of military spending, the financial resources of states would be better spent on ensuring human well-being, and, for many populations, even bare survival. According to UN estimates, starvation and the worst forms of malnutrition could be eliminated from the face of the Earth with an annual investment of about $19 billion; shelter could be provided for the world's homeless for $21 billion; clean water could be provided for everyone for about $10 billion; deforestation could be halted for $7 billion; global warming could be prevented for $8 billion, and soil erosion for $24 billion. Investing in such programs for a period of ten years would go a long way toward alleviating frustration and mitigating resentment in the world, and would prove far more effective in paving the way to stability and peace than funding military campaigns to attack "rogue" states and threaten uncooperative regimes.

The Neolithic Illusion, Social Darwinism, Market Fundamentalism, Consumerism, and Militarism are powerful beliefs we would be wise to forgo and forget. They need to be put on trial, subjected to impartial and objective scrutiny. As long as they dominate the minds of decision makers, and as long as there is no critical mass of new-thinking people in civil society, the dream of cocreating a peaceful, fair, and sustainable Akashic Age will remain nothing more than a dream.

5

THE RISE OF QUANTUM RESONANCE

The new thinking we need is not a miraculous gift, coming to us like manna from heaven. The basic tenets on which it rests need to be understood and given credence. Here science figures prominently. Whether we agree with it or not, science is a principal factor underlying credibility in the modern world. If it is "scientific," it is true, or it is likely to be true for its time. Thus, the challenge is to call attention to the view of the world emerging at science's cutting edge. This view could inform people's thinking and guide their steps. It has unparalleled and as yet largely unrecognized relevance to our life and times.

THE NEW PARADIGM IN SCIENCE: WHAT IT IS

Albert Einstein captured the objective of scientists in his well-known saying that scientists seek the simplest possible scheme that can tie together the facts they observe. This phrase encapsulates the quintessence of the project of fundamental science. Fundamental science is neither technology, nor discovery: it is understanding. This is of great practical relevance. When our understanding of reality matches the nature of reality, we discover more and more about the reality that underlies our life. We then have a greater ability to cope with our own place and role in the scheme of life. Understanding is fundamental.

Genuine science seeks the scheme that can convey comprehensive, consistent, and optimally simple understanding. That scheme is not established once and for all; it needs to be periodically updated. The observed facts grow with time and become more diverse. Tying them together in an optimally simple yet comprehensive scheme calls for revising and occasionally reinventing that scheme. In recent years, the repertoire of observed facts has grown and has become highly diverse. We need a new scheme: a new paradigm.

This is how science evolves: through alternating phases of what philosopher of science Thomas Kuhn called *normal science* and *revolutionary science*. Paradigm shifts are radical. Normal science treads water: it is only marginally innovative. It ties together the observed facts within an established scheme that is validated by consensus. If it encounters observations that do not fit that scheme, it extends and adjusts that scheme. This, however, is not always possible. If the attempt is not relinquished, the dominant scheme becomes unmanageably complex and opaque, as Ptolemaic astronomy did through the constant addition of epicycles to its basic cycles to account for the "anomalous" movement of the planets. When, in the growth of science, that critical point is reached, it is time to take a radical step. The dominant scheme must be scrutinized, discarded, and replaced. A new paradigm must be found to ground the theories and interpret the observations that support them.

In the natural sciences, a paradigm-shift point has now been reached. A number of unexpected—and, for the current paradigm, critically anomalous—observations have surfaced.

The series of critically anomalous observations can be traced to experimental findings that came to light in the early 1980s. A paper by French physicists Alain Aspect and collaborators reported on an experiment carried out under rigorously controlled conditions. This experiment was suggested by Einstein nearly half a century earlier. It involves splitting a particle and projecting the split halves some finite distance apart. Then some measurements are to be made on the distant halves. According to the "uncertainty principle" put forward by Erwin Schrödinger, we cannot observe all aspects of a particle at the same time; when we observe some, the others become blurred or go on to infinity. Einstein suggested that we can overcome this limitation by making observations on the split halves. If we can observe some of the parameters on certain ones and some on the others, we would observe both, and have overcome the strange limitations encapsulated in Schrödinger's principle. Aspect and collaborators managed to test the physical reality of this assumption and came up with a strange finding. It turned out that the split halves remain instantaneously connected over any finite distance. When we take a measurement on one half, it is as if we would have made that measurement on the other. The uncertainty principle holds even across space—and because the signal that connects the halves is instantaneous, it also holds over time. This, however, contradicts Einstein's own relativity theory, which holds that the maximum speed of propagation of anything across space is the speed of light.

Aspect's experiment was repeated, and always produced the same result. The scientific community was baffled, but finally dismissed the phenomenon as not having any deep significance: the "entanglement" of the split particles, physicists said, is strange, but it does not convey information or "do" anything. But this, too, was called into question in subsequent experiments. It turned out that the quantum state of particles, and even of whole atoms, can be instantly projected across any finite distance. This came to be known as "teleportation." Then instant quantum-resonance-based interactions were discovered in living systems, and even in the universe at large.

A related anomalous fact came to light in regard to the level and form of coherence found in complex systems. The observed coherence suggests "nonlocal" interaction between the parts or elements of the systems—interaction that transcends the recognized bounds of space and time. This kind of interaction surfaced not only in the quantum domain but, surprisingly, at the macroscopic level as well.

Yet another finding, inexplicable by the current paradigm, is that organic molecules are produced in stars. The received wisdom is that the universe is a physical system in which life is, if not an anomalous, at least a rare and most likely accidental phenomenon. After all, living systems can evolve only under conditions that are extremely rare in space and time. However, it turned out that the basic substances on which life is based are already produced in the evolution of stars. These are organic molecules, synthesized in the fiery process of stellar evolution and then ejected into surrounding space. They coat asteroids and clumps of interstellar matter, including those that subsequently fuse into stars and planets. It appears that the universe is remarkably well-tuned for life: its basic physical processes produce the very substances required for the evolution of living systems.

Observations of this kind are not amenable to being tied together by patching up the dominant scheme: they challenge not only the maximum velocity of effect propagation* in space, but our understanding of the most basic processes in nature. They call into question the paradigm of the Late Modern Age: the basic scheme by which contemporary scientists tie together the observed facts.

This is not the first revolution to rock science. An analogous revolution took place at the turn of the twentieth century, with the shift from the Newtonian to the relativity paradigm, and again in the 1920s with the advent of quantum theory. More limited revolutions have unfolded in specific domains since then, among them in psychology, with the emergence of transpersonal theories, and in cosmology, with the advent of non–Big Bang, multicyclical-universe models.

The next revolution promises to be even more fundamental. Relativity theory changed our notions of space and time, but the strange relativistic effects came to light only at speeds approaching that of light. The quantum revolution seemed to affect only the supersmall world in nature. The everyday world did not and does not seem to be affected by these revolutionary findings. But this limitation will not hold in the next paradigm shift. The new paradigm affects everything we see and know in and about the world.

---

*Effect-propagation is the transmission of a physical effect, such as heat or kinetic energy, from an open point in space or time—the cause—to another, which is the effect produced by the cause.

What is the new paradigm? Grasping it calls for a veritable Gestalt switch. We normally think of the things we experience as real, and the space that embeds them as empty and passive, a mere abstraction. We need to turn this around. It is the space that embeds things that is real, and the things that take place in space that are secondary. They are the manifestations of space. More precisely, they constitute the underlying generative and interconnecting matrix that fills space.

This concept emerges from the findings of cutting-edge physics. Space, quantum physicists now realize, is not empty and passive; it is a filled and active plenum, even though physicists still refer to it as the "quantum *vacuum*." In the emerging view, space is the ground, and the things we know as real things in the world are the figures on the ground. They are figures not just *on* a ground; they are figures *of* the ground. The things we consider real are manifestations of space—manifestations of the cosmic matrix that fills space.

There is a good metaphor for this concept of the world. Think of waves traveling over the surface of the sea. When you look at the surface, you see waves moving toward the shore, waves spreading out behind ships, waves colliding with waves. The waves move from one point on the sea toward another, yet there is nothing in the sea that would move that way: the molecules of water on the surface do not move from one place to another, they just move up and down. The motion of the waves is an illusion—an illusion not in the sense that there would be nothing that would correspond to it, but in that it is not what it appears to be. The waves travel across the surface of the sea, but the water of the sea does not travel.

The same applies to the motion of things in space. Things do not move *across* or *over* space, they move *in,* or more precisely *within,* space. They are *conveyed* by space. Space is not empty and passive: everything that exists in the world exists within the dimension of the world we call space.

The vision the emerging paradigm gives us is very different from the still-dominant vision. The world that meets our eye is not an illusion, but it is not what it appears to be, either. The real world is not an arena of separate things moving across intervening space. All things are part of that matrix, and are conveyed in and by the matrix. The bare existence of things is not the illusion; their separateness is. All things are *in* and *of* the matrix, and in the final count are *one* with the matrix.

Fantastic? No—it's science: quantum science. This world is a giant quantum system where all things, and not only supersmall, quantum things, are "entangled," intrinsically and instantly interconnected. Recognizing this is vital for our own well-being and for the survival of the whole of humanity. But first a word on what this concept does to our habitual picture of the world.

THE NEW PARADIGM IN SCIENCE: WHAT IT MEANS FOR OUR LIFE AND TIMES

Why is this new paradigm of such importance in regard to the thinking we need in our crisis-prone but rapidly evolving world? The answer is, first and foremost, because it gives us a sense of belonging. We are not separate individuals, pursuing our destiny in a strange, indifferent, and often hostile world. We belong to the world, and, in the final analysis, we are one with the world.

The Akashic paradigm turns our current picture of the world on its head. In the everyday context, we think that the things we see are real, and the space that embeds them is empty and passive. We now turn this around. It is the space that embeds things that is real, and the things that move about in space that are secondary. This is the deep dimension of the world the ancient rishis called *Akasha*. Their intuition is now confirmed at the cutting edge of the sciences.

The new Akashic paradigm is a holistic paradigm. All things interact with all other things, and all things are what they are through their interactions. Wholeness is the essence of the new concept of reality. The world is a coherent whole, made up of parts or elements coherently related each to the other.

The idea of *coherence* is fundamental. In any system, whether it is a molecule, a mouse, a human being, or a galaxy, the parts are finely tuned to one another: they respond to each other and to the rest of the world as one. They are instantly coherent. Life would not be possible in the absence of such coherence, nor would any other complex system. Ecologies need to be coherent to persist, and the web of life itself needs to be coherent. Only the societies of humans can exist in a state of partial incoherence, but they, too, cannot exist in that state for long. Incoherence in a system is unsustainable. It is at the root of the unsustainability of the human world in our time.

The holistic Akashic paradigm gives important guidance for us both individually and collectively. This guidance is based on the recognition that, since the coherence of the whole is a precondition of the functioning of the parts, maintaining the coherence of the whole is fundamental in sustaining a balanced system. When it comes to human beings, it is "the good"—that is, the right, the wise way to act and to be.

Coherence is not a purely individual attribute. The right way to act, and to be, is not merely to enhance our own, individual coherence, but to contribute to the coherence of the systems that sustain our life. This means safeguarding our coherence with our community, with the whole human community, and with the web of life that frames the whole human community. It calls for cooperation—embracing, systemwide cooperation.

Maintaining our individual coherence calls for cooperation between the cells and organs that make up our body. Despite the diversity of our cells and organs—indeed, *because of* and *through* their diversity— we can perform the almost miraculous feat of maintaining ourselves in life's inherently unstable state far from equilibrium. This feat is achieved because in a healthy organism all cells and organs are effectively and precisely coordinated. Any breakdown in coordination is a sign of weakness, a prelude to disease.

A healthy organism is organically coherent, with all its parts tuned together to maintain the system in its environment. But for achieving and maintaining organic coherence, coherence with others and with nature is sine qua non. Health for a living system requires both internal and external coherence.

In today's world, external coherence is highly constrained: many people act as if they were separate from the world around them. They behave as if the world and they were categorically distinct and different. This is an error, and it has grave consequences. People who feel they are separate are prone to treat others and their environment as a means to satisfy their own ends and aspirations without regard for the health and well-being of others, disregarding the coherence of the system that supports life on the planet. This is a dangerous condition. Species that possess a higher nervous system cannot follow this dangerous path—they are more intrinsically connected with the world around them and cannot sever or ignore their web of connections. We, on the other hand, can fail to recognize our ties with each other and with nature and entertain the illusion of separateness.

Recognizing the paramount importance of coherence is a key to our individual health and well-being, as well as to the survival of our species. The Akashic paradigm highlights this fact, not as an arbitrary moral command, but as the basic law of life and existence in the biosphere. It gives us a consistent view of ourselves, of nature, and of the cosmos. It is a key to recovering the harmony that traditional people felt with each other and with their environment.

We have lost our sense of oneness, but have not lost it irrevocably. With the new vision that emerges at the cutting edge of the sciences, we can lend credence to our suppressed but still vital sense of oneness and belonging: this is not an illusion. When all is said and done, we are truly one with each other, with the biosphere, and with the cosmos.

6

A CLOSER LOOK AT THE AKASHIC DAWN

Any viable vision for an Akashic Age must address the fact that we cannot continue along the way we have been going. Human civilization cannot continue along a path of increasing returns on a finite planet. Many of the current problems we face—in politics, trade, finance, energy, civil society, food, security, and the like—are exacerbated by the interdependency of our highly managed, worldwide infrastructures and the old-paradigm consciousness that drives them. In order to resolve the difficulties in our contemporary world, our global societies need to put in place the following:

- New forms of energy sources that can be adequately collected, distributed, and utilized and that are renewable. This will require a shift from finite to infinite energy sources, which are naturally produced and can be fairly distributed to maintain a global civilization.
- Ubiquitous global communications that allow fair and egalitarian access for all people to engage in free and open communication and connection worldwide.

Our vision of the years ahead involves a lot of ground shifting, as different aspects of change reshuffle and reassemble themselves. This period of uncertainty and unsettlement is the bottleneck we spoke of earlier. It is the preparatory effort that lays the groundwork for a new model to come into being—a model that acknowledges the planet's limits in resources and encourages individual and community well-being, rather than putting its faith in perpetual material abundant growth, coming to fruition in economics and consumerism. The rapid technological growth enabled by our fuel-rich preceding century and a half has enabled us to evolve, and test, a new scientific understanding. It has allowed us to travel, connect, and communicate across vast distances as never before.

Fortunately, our global expansion has been accompanied by an expansion of our awareness and empathy, and an epiphany. We have now arrived at a new crossroads in our civilizational journey. Now we need to make decisions based on the tools we have acquired. It is not about abandoning the usefulness and the knowledge from our past, but rather applying them in a manner that is more fitting for the way ahead. Like all generational knowledge handed down in history, we pass on the best from our epoch in order to infuse and inspire the succeeding one.

The developmental myth that has brought us to the tipping point of change is a paradigm of increasing industrialization, urbanization, and population growth. This way of thinking, in the West particularly, has promoted and rewarded an increasingly isolationist way of life. It is one where we struggle with a world separate from the self and compete to gain advantage over others. This is a story of separation that ignores the fact that our problems are interrelated.

This paradigm is no longer useful, and we see it losing its persuasive power in the second decade of the twenty-first century. As the years pass, more and more people will realize that the old paradigm is alienating, disempowering, and contributing to a path of decline. It is in this coming decade especially that we have the responsibility to usher in a new way of thinking and a new social narrative that will help the new epoch, the Akashic Age, to emerge.

To have a healthy and vibrant future means investing in people, in our communities, in our "We-ness." Writer Doris Lessing referred to this as the condition of SOWF—*Substance Of We Feeling*. As in the old gift economies, where goods and services were exchanged without monetary transaction or future rewards, intrinsic value comes through giving rather than looking after only oneself. In other words, value meant service to others above the limiting view of only service to self. We view the bottleneck of disruptions as being instrumental in bringing people and communities together through changing circumstances. The shifting focus can be used to catalyze self-exploration and innovative social experiments.

Young people have the capacity to reskill themselves, creating more content and meaning; this has already been happening with online content and collaborations such as YouTube, open-source software, and social networks and organizations. If and when people can no longer pay for things, they will start to create them, each of them according to their unique circumstances. We can leave behind the emphasis on a one-size-fits-all prescriptive model and steer toward local variations—assets, resources, and the like—that can stimulate the emergence of discoveries, activity, and creative solutions, depending on locations and available resources.

The local scale is the more robust, so the future needs to become inherently more local: an intentional movement toward local self-dependency. Such arrangements could include local forms of currency, locally managed community energy, local food production and distribution, and local social enterprises (as we discuss later in this chapter). The extensive technologies of communication and connectivity that we currently enjoy can, and need to be, maintained and sustained as a priority so that local regions and communities can not only stay connected but also collaborate and share skills and resources. What we see here is the rise of localized hubs operating within global networks. These localized hubs involve communities that are self-defining, self-organizing collectives that share resources. Localization is, after all, also the celebration of place. People can be proud of local development and self-sufficiency, regardless of their political ideologies.

As the global economy further contracts, our energy-fueled mobility could begin to be replaced by strongly local "living economies" that emphasize local resources, knowledge, and skills. As regions shift their focus onto what they are able to provide, such as local goods and food, this could stimulate a reinvigoration of distinct local cultures. A surge in local growth and resilience would be supported by our global connections and technologies of communication. Such networks would also facilitate a move away from "heavier" technologies (i.e., energy intensive and more centrally controlled) toward distributed networks that require less energy to sustain them. Heavy technology, such as our current transport systems, will need to be thoroughly redesigned in order to mesh with future alternative energy sources. As we will discuss shortly, heavily centralized utility infrastructures need to be replaced by horizontal, decentralized, and distributed networks.

We are not talking about going back to a more primitive state. Rather, we are talking about adopting an integral Akashic view that is more enriching and empowering for people—one that supports a sustainable future. We are talking about engaging with people's passion for change, rather than with their fear.

A globally aligned response, through utilizing local resources and assets, may be a way of fostering coherence throughout society. The Akashic Age can be nourishing and enticing, inspiring voluntary involvement rather than coercion.

No longer can we pursue the business-as-usual model, as this will crash us into a great wall. And, although the road to increasing local self-dependency may not be as easy and cheerful a path as we may like to believe, it will eventually be to our advantage. The hard work involved in doing things differently can also offer to us a deeper appreciation of our human connections—our matrix of family, friends, and neighbors—as well as the satisfaction of acquiring new capacities and learning new skills.

As evolutionary biologists tell us, there comes a time in species development and growth when the necessity to collaborate, rather than compete, becomes not only an advantage, but an evolutionary imperative. The signs of this greater connectivity of sharing have been unfolding within our modern cultures over some years now. This greater connectivity will be instrumental in creating our humane and sustainable communities as the Akashic Age dawns.

SHARING OUR CONNECTIONS

A new form of participatory consciousness has been emerging through our increased interconnectivity and global communications. This is a distributed model that connects people in a more egalitarian way, rather than through centralized structures. It catalyzes people into becoming more active through their participation. No longer do we have to be members of the passive audience, as we were during the earlier communication revolutions of radio and television. The new model, already with us, involves blogging, cell-phone text messaging, social networking, and engaging in similar forms of decentralized social media. The dialogue is now shifting into a more active domain, where people are putting themselves onstage and orchestrating their own connections, presence, and self-expression. At the dawn of the Akashic Age, the civil body of the planet will really began to grow and expand its reach.

Social networks—both physical and virtual—have matured tremendously over recent years, with the list of global nongovernmental organizations (NGOs) growing longer, and stronger, with each passing year. These innovative networks are the forums for visionary thinkers, where new ideas and concepts can spread virally through the communications-based nervous system of the planet.

The new civil body of social networking that joins individuals together worldwide is set to become a major feature of an integrated planetary society. With talks being broadcast regularly online, access to an array of innovative lectures, and social forums, people can be actively influenced, and alternative thinking and ideas can be stimulated. A more mature form of collective social intelligence can begin to emerge in various parts of the globe. Indeed, we envision that civil society, which is the largest movement in history, will grow to become more dominant and influential in transforming our societies. To belong to this diverse and yet unified family is not only a responsibility, it is also a blessing.

The new contours of connection and communication are predisposed to a nonhierarchical, bottom-up format: this is the essence of functional models for the Akashic Age. These are peer-to-peer collaborative models, generating greater individualization within a shared, complex, diverse yet unified field of interaction. This form of networked unity will make the old model obsolete.

Externally we may seem to be a vast, distant, and separated collection of people, yet reality is just the opposite. The reality is that we form a dense, intimate, closely entwined species of various races, sharing a nonlocal sense of being. Younger generations of people worldwide are growing up with a new expression of consciousness. Recent explorations of the human psyche—psychological, psychoanalytical, transpersonal, and so on—are mixing with technologies of communication and connection that herald a more reflexive mode of thought. Younger people are increasingly more comfortable in expressing themselves with strangers. Many of them explore and express their inner thoughts, feelings, emotions, and ideas with hundreds of unknown people online, from various cultural backgrounds. More and more daily interactions are empathic, as people react to and share news, stories, and emotional impacts from sources around the world.

Empathy is becoming one of the core values by which we create and sustain social life. Exposure to impacts outside our own narrow environment will help us to achieve tolerance. We are living with experiences that are richer and more complex, full of ambiguities, multiple realities, and shared perceptions. This is a way of constructing more social capital in this world. It is a model that was used in ancient communities, where cultural capital preceded commercial capital. Cultural relations were primary and came before commercial relations, and they focused on social benefit, rather than profit. We see this happening today in myriad incarnations, thanks to open-source collaborative tools, such as Wikipedia, where a global commons for sharing can develop above the individual drive for profit and commercial gain.

Millions of online friendships have already been formed, and this trend is likely to increase. Every day, online social networks create thousands of friendships, even across conflicting religions and regions. The online worlds of social networking are often fueled by genuine empathy and a spirit of sharing. Around the world an hour of video is now uploaded every second; we are collectively generating more content than ever before in the history of civilization. In the years ahead, these social networks may become our principal channels of communication, whereby individuals gain almost instant access to news occurring in other areas around the world, bypassing traditional modes of mainstream news media. Social networks of friendships have the potential to become our news service, as we rely more on trusted friendships than mainstream media.

According to Google CEO Eric Schmidt we are now creating in two days as much information as we did from the dawn of civilization up until 2003 and that by 2013 that quantity of information will be created every ten minutes. Most of this is user-generated content—material that people have created themselves and contributed to the world. It is estimated that more than 68 million users share content every day. As an example of the figures involved, more video is uploaded to YouTube every six months than was produced by the three major U.S. TV networks in the past sixty years.

What is emerging is an incredible global platform for sharing, in large part free of commercial ambitions. The online encyclopedia Wikipedia is a shining example of this—a free resource with over 13 million articles monitored and maintained by tens of thousands of volunteers worldwide. Between them, they have donated more than 100 million hours of time to creating it. If it were a book, Wikipedia would be 2.25 million pages long—and it is given free for all to use as they wish.

All of this makes for an stupendous platform for connecting ideas and content, with very little personal investment in skills and finance. This collaborative and participatory world of online content could become a "global commons" that reinforces a sense of local identity while connecting people in all parts of the globe. This outreach of connectivity has the power and the potential to break down old perceptual paradigms of duality—the us and them—that have been exploited by governments and ruling authorities to serve their own goals of control and conquest.

We are increasingly exposed to each other in ways without precedent. The children born in the new millennium—sometimes referred to as Millennials—are growing up embedded within virtual social networks that transcend space and time, as well as cultures, national boundaries, and local ideologies.

The younger generations are accustomed to sending and receiving information in a way that could nourish local networks, rather than replacing them. This can prompt increasing numbers of young people from many nations to become involved in community and social projects and with NGOs—for example, by taking a year out of their lives to help in another culture abroad, to learn and experience new things, and to offer assistance where needed.

Volunteering among the young is on the rise. With this pattern increasing in the coming years, social networks can become a major source of cultural education, helping young people to learn tolerance, appreciation, and respect for their fellow human beings. The world's young generation (Generation Y) is coming of age at a critical time when it can help create a new world through networks of sharing. The young generation, which has an open playing field before them, can foster collaboration, generosity, and communication. Instead of being labeled as Generation Y (Why?), they have the potential to become Generation BE.

The model that the Internet and other distributed communications represent is a bottom-up, decentralized medium for spreading awareness, information, and contact. It is a horizontal medium in that it bypasses the old model of top-down, hierarchical control structures that have been so rigidly in place in recent history. If it is to truly become an effective new model for the Akashic Age, this horizontal model of decentralized connectivity needs to grow and develop beyond the virtual world into the physical world. It must be able to transform how we do things daily in our communities and immediate environments. The applications of the model need to cross-fertilize, so that our technologies of global connectivity could enhance and enrich our lives, friendships, and connections.

If we are to move into a sustainable, harmonious, and vibrant future, our leading-edge technologies have to be designed and used for transforming, nourishing, and improving our everyday lives and changing the way we do business. In the coming years, we need to start putting such models into place. A positive vision of the Akashic Age compels us to democratize our thinking and our ways of acting.

DEMOCRATIZING THE WAY WE DO THINGS

The conventional way of doing things—"business as usual"—has, at least since the recent modernization of our societies, been based on the centralization of supply and distribution. It is time for this traditional form of hierarchical organization of economic and political power to be replaced by a distributive model that fosters connection and collaboration, rather than control and competition. As the population shifts to encompass a greater proportion of those who have been accustomed to social media networking, with an emphasis on collaboration and increased transparency, it could usher in a major shift, a transformation in how we do things, how we relate to others, but also in the very way our minds work—in consciousness itself. As we explore throughout this chapter and the next, a transition from vertical to horizontal/lateral connections has the potential to empower collaborative creative development in such areas as civil society, energy, economy, politics, education, and more. These changes will enable the emergence of the Akashic Age on our planet.

In recent years we have seen an increase in how information and communication is becoming democratized: from corporate whistle-blowers to Wikileaks; online e-book sharing, alternative press, social forums, civil movements, distributed commerce, and the like. This revolution-in-the-making may have a greater impact on people socially and culturally than did the print revolution of the fifteenth century, brought on by Johannes Gutenberg.

What is beginning to manifest here is a model based on shared interest as opposed to self-interest. It is a model that emphasizes the collective power of many interconnections over the centralized few. It is no coincidence then that in these transitional years we are seeing clashes emerging between the vested interests of the status quo (political and financial elites) and the decentralized yet empowered and activated general public (civil society). We witnessed many of these clashes occurring throughout 2011 and 2012 (Arab Spring, the Indignant Movement, the Occupy Movements, etc.), and we will see many more of them in the days, months, and years ahead. Yet these clashes, which are likely to mark the coming years, can be catalysts for cocreating new worldviews that can then stabilize and become the newly accepted paradigm for thinking and acting.

The underlying ethic is simple and yet it is difficult to adjust to for those accustomed to individual struggle in competitive societies. This ethic is based on the emerging holistic insight that contributing to the well-being of the whole also increases one's individual well-being. It is an age-old, indeed timeless, insight. It lends meaning to the concept of reciprocal maintenance. Those who are able to adapt well to collaborative ideals, such as the Internet generation, can better resist the old paradigm of centralized governance, surveyed borders, and controlled supply chains. Such collaborative ideals seek a more open, transparent, and borderless world that reflects the way decentralized communications are operating. The young people of the future may well ask their older peers why the centralized monopolies of the past fought for control over the Earth's resources. For these younger people, the planet's resources are a public good to be shared by all.

Old thinking will seem anachronistic, a matter of fruitless greed, to those who grow up within our new era of communication and collaboration. The decade ahead is a crucial time when there is great potential for growth in collaborative interactions, community building, creativity and shared ideas, social capital and entrepreneurship, empathy and tolerance, and equal access to global networks.

The playing field needs to be shifted from one that is vertical, centralized, and controlled, to a field that is horizontal, distributed, and inclusive. The Internet will be crucial in opening up this new lateral field. It has already shown that people can do things without the middleman, or even without permission from the top. People are being encouraged to form, foster, and develop their own creative networks and communities.

With millions of people now having the opportunity to connect together and form direct relationships, a whole new era of cottage industries could spring up. Within the next decade, there could be many thousands of people working from home, supplying individualized items direct to clients worldwide, earning personal feedback, and developing direct producer-customer relations. A multitude of similar projects could be created around this model, in all areas and interests, combining virtual with physical networks and relations, to form a new culture based on a distributive-collaborative paradigm.

(R)EVOLUTIONS IN FOOD

Part of the dawning Akashic Age must surely be for people to create and develop their own food (r)evolutions, both rural and urban, by forming communities that can learn to grow their own food through neighborhood gardening, cooking, and composting programs. These communities can then connect with networks of local farmers' markets and other community-supported agriculture programs, such as vertical gardening (planting on walls in space-restricted environments).

As we alluded to previously, our reliance on industrial agriculture has resulted in a food supply riddled with hidden environmental, economic, and health care costs. Further, with a large part of our global food chain managed by a handful of corporate giants that supply the major food supermarkets, we are incredibly vulnerable to supply-chain disruption. Add to this the potential for environmental disruption to our centralized food-production regions, and we have a recipe for food shortages and unpredictable cost increases. On top of this, we must also acknowledge that much food nowadays is simply not healthy for the human body.

What is important is for local communities and urban neighborhoods to establish local centers not only for food production but also for local storage and distribution. What it comes down to is the availability of and access to information and knowledge. By utilizing both local word of mouth and also via the Internet, people can learn about gardening workshops, self-farming techniques, and how to start urban gardens and homesteading. Neighborhoods can also begin to source their own water supplies and introduce local permaculture schemes. Social networks can be established to bring home gardeners together to share tips, advice, and friendship. Modern gardening movements could help redefine regional food production for the next decade, with local representatives discussing and sharing sustainable alternatives to industrial agriculture. These networks could then collaborate together to encourage and develop a postindustrial food system that is less resource-intensive and more locally based and managed.

Similarly, new networks of investors, donors, entrepreneurs, farmers, and activists—all committed to building local food systems and local economies—could form part of the new set of change agents. For example, farmers could begin shifting to a distributed farming model whereby people pledge an investment to the farmer before the growing season in order to then receive a share of the crops throughout the year. This form of responsible sharing, and investing, benefits not only one's well-being but also the well-being of the local food producer (that is, the farmer). It demonstrates how producers and consumers could be directly connected in a participatory and democratic model within the food chain.

Such projects, and many more like them, could catalyze the growth of localized and regionalized cooperatives. Furthermore, out of this could grow food and agriculture groups that begin to teach people about both urban and rural homesteading, perhaps even sending out advisors/teachers to visit local areas and train others. A whole mobile network of grow-your-own-food advisors could become a part of responsible citizenry in the years ahead. This could become crucial for the large numbers of people who, over the years, have moved into the cities, and who now find themselves looking to forge a more sustainable lifestyle. The shift from an industrial mode to a collaborative era could take place over the next decade(s) and prove highly beneficial to urban areas.

DEMOCRATIZING THE FUTURE

This distributive model can be developed in urban environments through cooperative car clubs and car-sharing schemes. In the past few years, car sharing has significantly developed in many countries in Europe, North America, and Asia as cities face increasing residential parking problems and associated congestion. For example, Zipcar (founded in 2000) is now the world's largest car-sharing business, and has hundreds of thousands of members and several thousand locations around the world. While still used by a minority of people, these collaborative schemes could become the norm by fostering a consciousness of shared use, rather than the old-mind model of ownership and possession. People in urban locations need no longer purchase a car outright, but could make use of a wide-ranging selection of services that emerge to offer shared-transport facilities. This could also apply for regular routes, such as airport runs. Not only would this help to lessen energy use and transport pollution, but it would also bring many people together and help to forge new sharing networks and friendships.

New friendship networks could very well become crucial to shifting into a collaborative Akashic Age. Similar to the new global network called Couchsurfing—an online service that connects travelers to host houses in countries all over the world—an array of networking services could prove successful in turning online networks into real-life physical encounters and friendships.

New community friendship networks could help young people travel across the world cheaply, instead of relying on hotels and hostels. As in Couchsurfing, people across the world would open their homes to host travelers from other countries. Such networks could also greatly assist people, especially the young, in forging new connections with people of similar ages that could develop into other social projects. These forms of creative collaboration would not come from the center, as major commercial enterprises with huge promotions, but would emerge from the fringe. That is, quietly, without fanfare, yet gaining members at exponential rates.

These models could make the early adopters into a new wave of disruptive innovators. *Disruptive innovation* refers to initiatives that are unexpected and arrive, usually from the periphery or fringe, to provide services that have previously been monopolized. An example of this would be online music downloading and sharing, which initially rocked the traditional music publishing industry. Such disruptions are highly threatening to the hierarchical status quo, yet they can be empowering to civil society. There is already much disruptive innovation taking place around the world, with many "tinkerers" searching for solutions beneficial for people, rather than for profit. This trend could very well be part of the new Akashic Age emerging in the years ahead. This would mark a shift of the social sphere away from consumerism and capitalist exploitation and toward self-empowerment and community sustainability. The young social entrepreneurs arising within this new Akashic consciousness would change how power operates and is managed, thereby catalyzing sustainable economic and social models.

When we look back at the classical system that consisted of the industrial extraction of fossil fuels, constructing superhighways of concrete, installing heavy cables, developing global trade zones, centralizing business into conglomerates, and the like, we see now how fixed, monopolized, and energy-intensive this system has been. Yet it was necessary in forming and developing our diverse societies into a planetary body of interconnections. Now that we have formed our global tentacles we are able to shift into an era whereby more intensely localized economies can be sustained; they can keep us connected, informed, and creatively inspired.

In the coming years, we could start to see a shift toward an era of open planetary dialogue as information and communications become even more democratized, accessible, and widely shared. However, this shift toward the Akashic Age may well ignite resistance, as democratic access to globally shared information will be hard fought over as the old guard struggles to retain their control. Yet the new paradigm emerging today could encourage the emergence of a model that blends more localized ways of living with increased planetary awareness and a consciousness of our shared humanity. Such a new social paradigm would involve increased creative collaboration between individuals and communities; the support of local products and services; the reusing and bartering model replacing the consume and throwaway culture; and a commitment to strengthening our community relations.

While living through the coming years of austerity and financial uncertainties, we can be inspired to become more connected, communicative, and appreciative of our relationship with the natural world. In doing so we begin to participate in cocreating a more sustainable, equitable, and meaningful future for us all.

7

NEW AKASHIC MODELS

Moving toward the Akashic Age means leaving behind an old era predicated on a century and a half of unprecedented growth, competition, and selfish drive. The new Akashic models that we can assist in birthing are ones that embrace the finer connections of conscious communication, collaboration, and service to others. These are models that focus less on consumption of goods and more on information, knowledge skills, support, guidance, and the exchange of services without monetary transaction. These are the lighter forms of transaction; that is, they are not centralized, overtly controlled, or energy intensive. As such, they can be distributed and shared more easily.

The First and Second Industrial Revolutions excluded the so-called developing countries, as industrial nations leaped ahead with highways, cables, armies, and controlled trade routes. In the coming years, we may find that the once-developing nations are able to leapfrog into the new era by participating in the growing global commons and distributed networks. The upcoming reshuffling between political models has the potential to shift from being polarized between left and right ideologies, and instead redefine itself by being inclusive and cooperative, rather than exclusive and divisive. Already, regional networks have been created as nation-states expand into regional blocs: EU (European Union), AU (African Union), UNASUR (Union of South American Nations), AL (Arab League), and ASEAN (Association of Southeast Asian Nations), to name but a few.

For example, in 2008 the African Union initiated the Africa-Europe

Energy partnership (AEEP), where just under $130 million was pledged to developing and promoting sustainable energy projects.[1] The rise in collaborative energy projects may well stimulate and encourage increased regional networking. The future is about forming and sustaining new alliances and international networks of fair and equitable trade. These can exist if there are also nonpolitical and neutral civil organizations to monitor their transparent operations. We need to insist that the future of international treaties of cooperation and collaboration are conducted as transparently as is possible, with negotiations open to external observers.

Nations that were once considered less developed are now becoming global players—such as China and India—and nations/regions that have abundant natural resources—including Russia, Iran, and Brazil—are forming new alliances. South America, for example, has agreed to forge stronger networking ties to protect its nations' own resources and develop local agreements of sustainable development. Member nations of the Union of South American Nations (UNASUR) have agreed to establish a South American parliament, to issue a single passport, to create a common currency, and to move toward an integrated, single market, initially by as early as 2014. In many of these countries, the younger generations will be expected to encourage and push for implementing a more democratic approach to economic, social, and political models.

Such countries as China, with a heavily centralized political structure, may ironically end up developing the very software and hardware that will be used to transform our global infrastructures of connectivity. As in the metaphor of the Trojan Horse, the very infrastructures that some countries are using to control their populations may be used as channels to connect and empower their people. The years ahead can be a time where many new minds are able to confront shared problems through connecting together rather than working alone. The tipping points toward change could well be marked by the vision of diversity within unity—the many working together to find solutions to both local and global problems.

Such new models would emerge as a reaction against the current westernized globalization model. They would foster cross-border collaborations, just as our recent revolutions in communications and consciousness have become nonlocal in aspect. Networks of communication, finance, energy, and trade would give rise to new interconnected arrangements, leading toward an increasingly integrated human society that at the same time would develop stronger regionally sustainable practices.

THE NEW ECONOMIES

In the next decade, we could witness many competitive markets coming under increasing pressure to give way to collaborative networks, both as an antidote to present woes and in reaction to social and technological forces. Over time the vertical top-down model of capitalism could find itself more and more marginalized by the emerging trends of distributed capital. That is, there may be a less-than-smooth transition as early adopters shift from existing forms of capitalism (markets dominated by the big players) to more participatory models of capitalism where people engage in small-scale direct lender-borrower relations. This represents the ongoing shift toward more democratic models; as the centralized control of global space—information, mobility, knowledge, and the like—is pushed toward borderless networks and shared connections. This would further transform the world into an energetically empowered global commons.

The dawn of the Akashic Age could very well see us entering the era of distributed economics. A distributed economy is one that focuses more on a regional-localized approach and seeks to promote innovation within small- and medium-size enterprises. It also has a strong emphasis upon sustainable investment and development. Distributed economics also encourages participation from alternative markets and would be flexible to disruptive innovation (see above). The early signs of this transition are already appearing. Consider the disputes involving the economy of access (such as in the download piracy acts), which are being played out in the music and film industry. The rights of access, and of information copyright, will initially become a disputed area as a distributed economy emerges, one that operates differently from the private-property mentality and model of current capitalism.

The transition to an Akashic Age acknowledges these disputes yet calls for people to creatively develop networks of sharing (music, films, media) that circumvent these old-model copyrights and terms of access. Any new model must make the old one obsolete yet should not engage in direct conflict. It is the responsibility of imaginative and innovative minds to collaborate on ways of sharing content and information that do not clash with preexisting laws. The new models, or systems, must be clean, conflict-free, and not on a collision course with the status quo. The shift needs to be toward an information currency standard, where the trading of information, knowledge, skills, time, services, advice, and guidance gains greater value and shared worth.

Traditional industries are proving too slow to deal with the forms of transaction that are likely to be part of this transition. This includes the phenomenal rise in music downloading, movie streaming, peer-to-peer sharing, and e-books. Users are now connecting directly with providers and the middlemen are becoming increasingly obsolete. We see this in online marketplaces (such as eBay), and many similar sites that connect providers with end users. The same is happening in finance and loans, as an array of social lending sites have arisen, such as Zopa, RateSetter, Prosper, P2P Financial, and others, to carve out a niche in distributed finance. As traditional financial institutions either collapse or become discredited, they may be replaced by online financial networks that connect funders with those requesting money in what could become a whole new model of economic exchange. The flexibility of such direct models could allow people to both request loans, at specific rates, as well as setting loan rates. This could also work as part of a community-funding model, whereby members of a community become responsible for funding local projects that add to their overall cohesion and sense of well-being. Investing in people, in community relations, and in local economic needs would be a more beneficial use of financial assets than traditional banking.

We can see how the rise of direct financial services—referred to here as distributed capital—could easily bypass traditional banks and brokerage houses. This model could further develop what is now emerging as crowd funding (also called crowd financing), whereby projects are proposed online and pledges/donations from the public are called for. People are able to donate as little or as much as they wish, and are able to follow the progress of their funded project. Crowd funding has met with success in many areas, including music artists seeking financial support from fans, independent filmmakers seeking production funds, funding for start-up companies, disaster relief, citizen journalism, political and environmental campaigns, and more. Early site adopters of this distributed-funding model include ArtistShare, Sellaband, Spot.Us, Kickstarter, and Crowdrise, among others.

Collaborative funding empowers users and places them in a more direct relationship to how their money and/or nonmonetary contributions are utilized. These transactions are also usually much more transparent, as the recipient of funds feels obligated to show how the funds are being used. In this way the receivers are empowered: they have the flexibility to proceed with their project outside of traditional financial-industry pressures.

These systems could, in the years ahead, become a major feature of how people increasingly connect among themselves to initiate and develop new creative projects. Millions of people disillusioned with mainstream capital markets could start to move into direct-to-user sponsoring and funding that allows them to feel a part of the project itself. This would usher in a new model of utilizing the "power of the many" to help spread the utility of money. This could help bring back a sense of meaningful transactions in economic relations—a true sense of participation in the energetic exchange of commerce and capital.

This concept of utilizing monetary transactions for well-being could be a catalyst for the renewed growth in the use of local currencies. Local currencies are complementary currencies that promote regional community investment and help to keep money local. Instead of being profit-oriented, they are use-oriented, which means they foster local transactions and support community enterprises. Complementary "local" currencies are easier to set up through transparent processes that allow users to see how their use benefits the community. This supports people and businesses that are part of a person's daily interactions.

Local money is a Depression-era idea and helps to tie in local consumers with their neighborhood suppliers. It works by local businesses and/or communities printing money and then users exchanging national currencies for the locally issued currencies and redeeming them in participating stores. The Totnes Pound, the Detroit Cheers, and the Bia Kut Chum are early-adopter models that have been used to buy goods and services in their communities. Recently, the city of Bristol, in the U.K., launched its own local currency with the slogan "Our City, Our Money." The scheme allows people to exchange national currencies for Bristol Pounds, which can be used to purchase goods and services at Bristol Pound–member businesses, either with the notes themselves, or via text by mobile phone or over the Internet.

The increasing use of local currency helps to keep money circulating among the community and encourages interaction and a sense of proximity between people and neighborhoods. This can also be extended for use in regional complementary currencies. This would help to establish a more circulation-based, ecological, use-oriented value of money. The idea of "ecological economics," which supports local currency schemes, would also help to encourage the emergence of barter and gift economies.

A gradual shift away from centralized financial capital toward public networks that promote social capital would encourage and strengthen relationships and collaborations, rather than ownership and property. It is also about whom you know and whom you are connected to, in terms of both physical and virtual networks. In an era of access and collaboration, sharing replaces ownership.

The Akashic Age will foster sharing and investing in one's communities. This also means an increased emphasis on supporting and investing in local entrepreneurs; that is, in people who have innovative ideas to solve social problems, whose solution benefits one's region as well as the greater good. The old model of centralized competition only favors the few to the detriment of the majority, and often bypasses communities and local well-being. The promotion and development of local projects and businesses adds a sense of empathy with people and commitment to place.

Recent years have seen the rise of "social entrepreneurs" who choose to channel great amounts of wealth into socially responsible projects that support social, cultural, and environmental goals. One example is eBay founder Pierre Omidyar, who established the Omidyar Network in 2004 that has so far committed over $290 million to support economic betterment worldwide. To promote the shift toward supporting social capital, we can envision a new wave of philanthropists who are young, idealistic, highly connected with the world, and who want to make a difference. Whereas classic philanthropy has often been seen as limited to the donor's own environment, with those who "made good" by giving back to their old neighborhood or city, by constructing museums and libraries, for example, the young philanthropists of today are deeply embedded in a connected world. Many of these people don't wish to simply donate money; they prefer to create innovations that can transform the world and benefit others. These emerging change agents have the capacity to catalyze and stimulate change, and are not risk-averse. In many cases, they are free to think outside the box, away from conventional wisdom, because they are not constrained by politics (as are politicians), or by shareholders (as are CEOs), nor do they need to spend a lot of time on fund-raising (as do professionals at NGOs). With greater numbers of younger people creating successful lives from a world that is literally at their fingertips, there can be greater investment in creative innovations seeking to cocreate a more sustainable and equitable future.

For businesses to stay competitive within the new economic model, they will be forced to invest more not only in the well-being of their employees but also in the wider community in which they operate. Due to the increasing awareness of the inequality of global trade tariffs and monopolies, people demand fair trade and ethical business practices. Further, people are able to create social movements in protest if they feel such objectives are not being met.

Social pressure, especially through burgeoning social media, could become a major voice in calling for businesses to invest in their communities, their employees' well-being, their environmental legacy, and consumer protection. Social media monitoring can also increasingly demand that companies internalize and absorb costs, instead of passing them on to the consumer. Economist Hazel Henderson has suggested, for example, that nation-states shift from taxing income to taxing resource depletion and pollution. Also, Henderson has suggested that tariffs be employed to support those countries that implement sustainable policies so as to remain competitive. Furthermore, she has proposed that a transaction tax (1 percent or less) be put into place for businesses, which could then use that money for funding nonprofit microfinancing initiatives.[2] The ever-visible voice of the people's social media can highlight and call for such changes, becoming a force that shifts the emphasis more and more toward social capital, rather than toward financial capital.

In the dawning Akashic Age, civil society could be the high-growth area where many of our young people gain meaning and fulfillment in their lives. The younger generations especially, growing up within the shared spaces of social networks, are likely to find greater resonance within civil society roles that favor empathic relations over financial ones.

As our current global economic models go through further transition, this could catalyze younger people to search out civil society roles that are better suited to an emerging global consciousness. We could have a future that puts less emphasis on its measure of national economic wealth (GDP), and more on such indices as the Index of Economic Well-Being (IEWB), the UN's Human Development Index (HDI), and Bhutan's Gross National Happiness (GNH) index. In the years to come, we could move toward celebrating the well-being of a society as meaning much more than just its economic performance. This means a future where economic models are more closely aligned with overall social well-being, including access to health and clean water, environmental impact, and education.

ALTERNATIVE ENERGY MODELS

Global energy corporations have largely shied away from major investments in renewable energy technologies in order to maintain their current energy model. This serves to maintain control and consumer confidence in the fossil-fuel industry. Fossil fuels have become locked in to the modern way of life. That is, particular ways of doing things become fixed and form part of a reinforcing pattern that affects behavior, products, industries, and forms of social life for decades. So many vested interests have their assets tied in with particular systems that they will do anything to maintain that system, even if it is inefficient. It is very difficult to break away from patterns that are not only ingrained within an array of related industries but are also accepted as the norm in the psychology of the masses. Yet this old model may be replaced by one emerging from the periphery, and driven by distributed networks, interconnectivity, and sustainability. As it becomes more obvious that the current model cannot go on for the long term, various global energy corporations will start making economic investments in new sources and markets as a sound business model. Once the shift begins, we can expect to see more business/corporate interests changing course in order to ride the new wave and not to miss out on capitalizing on the transition that will come about in any case.

According to the International Energy Agency (IEA), in order to keep oil production at a flat rate, slightly below 70 million barrels per day (to avoid a steep economic decline),* it would require an $8 trillion investment over the next twenty-five years to exploit the remaining oil deposits that are more difficult and expensive to extract and refine. On top of these initial costs are the huge financial and military investments needed to secure access to the fossil-fuel fields and to protect the thousands of miles of pipelines in order to deliver the fuel to the end users. This is an incredibly costly model of source and distribution that, by its very nature, requires a strong, centralized control system of management. It will be increasingly less profitable to continue investing in fossil fuels. The energy returned on energy invested (EROEI) equation will begin to favor searching out and developing new energy sources for the future.

What then does this tell us about potential new energy markets opening up, especially in how energy could be distributed in the short-term future? As our awareness of living on a small planet with finite resources grows, we could see increased interest, efforts, and investments in developing

---

*According to the International Energy Agency, global peak production of crude oil probably occurred in 2006 at 70 million barrels per day (bpd).

alternative nonfinite sources of power. The fallacy of perpetual growth fueled by finite energy sources can be replaced by a new model that combines all three factors: energy, technology, and ecological awareness. The Fukushima nuclear disaster after a tsunami hit Japan on March 11, 2011, is likely to put a halt to developing nuclear energy as a future power source. As they say, nuclear reactors are the world's most expensive and dangerous steam engines. Instead, such events could catalyze more research and emphasis on solar power, wind- and water-generated energy, geothermal energy, magnetic energy, and possibly, in the longer term, fusion power.

Our sun, as a solar generator, will always be there for us; thus, there will always be the potential for at least minimal power. On a hot, sunny day at noon, for example, the sun sends down roughly one kilowatt for every square meter of ground. The sum of this power falling on the Sahara alone, during one day-night cycle, is 3 million billion watts, or two hundred times greater than the present energy needs of civilization.[3] Nobel physicist Robert Laughlin notes that "even if we subtract 50 percent of this power due to inefficiency of solar panels and then another 10 percent through transmission loss . . . it would still be many times more than the world's energy needs."[4]

In recent years there has been a boost in investments in desert real estate, for building state-of-the-art solar farms. This includes the Chinese, who are pouring millions into alternative energy sources. The Chinese government has invested in a huge, 2-billion-watt solar park to be built in Inner Mongolia as part of its wind, solar, biomass, and hydroelectric energy growth. On a similar tack, the Japanese Trade Ministry announced a plan to investigate the feasibility of space solar power (SSP). This means placing huge solar-radiating satellites in Earth orbit 22,000 miles in space. Likewise, a consortium of Japanese companies have been in talks to join a $10 billion project aimed at launching a solar power station into space to generate billions of watts of power that could be beamed back to Earth. The urgency of such projects is now more evident than ever.

There is great potential in developing solar power, as it is a resource available over huge swaths of land, regardless of national boundaries. Solar power is available to countries regardless of their industrial development, which makes it an ideal area for future investment. Solar power generators can also be built for a vast range of uses, including larger regional and industrial use, moving down the scale all the way to community and household use. Governments need to subsidize solar energy to make it affordable for small businesses and households to invest in their own small-scale solar generators. So far this area has been sadly underfunded, even in countries with a high proportion of sunlight. As the years unfold, we need to see emerging markets in small-scale, low-end, solar power generators employed in communities and individual households.

Similarly, there are also many projects under way to develop wind power, especially in the European Union, where it is predicted to provide nearly 17 percent of the electricity for the EU by 2020, and 35 percent by 2030.[5] Generating energy from wind power grew globally from 17 billion watts in 2000 to 121 billion watts in 2008, as new wind turbine technology is now making it a more viable and profitable option.[6] Many countries in both Europe and Asia are investing heavily in wind power as an alternative energy source. One example of this is the Atlantic Wind Connection (AWC), which is planning to create a vast array of wind farms off the mid-Atlantic coast with hundreds of miles of these wind farms being connected and networked under the sea.

Similarly, tidal- and wave-generated power are seen as viable alternatives, especially since some of the largest and most populated cities on Earth are near the ocean. Undersea turbines are able to harness tide energies, capturing flowing water that can provide up to eight times more energy than wind. It is also possible to produce turbines that are scaled down to harness hydroelectric power from rivers in local areas and thus to provide for on-site power in rural locations. An extra incentive is that such a natural power source presents no danger to people living close by.

Again, these early-adopter programs in harnessing the world's natural energy sources need to shift up a gear. The areas that can benefit from both wind and tidal power include rural locations as well as large urban regions. There are many inland waterways running through urban and rural areas that could be utilized to become part of the tipping point in how we develop local energy sources.

Wind power, too, has the potential to produce energy on a range of scales, from the massive wind turbines we see on our landscapes, to smaller community and household use. The tipping point can be encouraged partly by a change in people's perceptions—by seeing the places and buildings where they live as energy sources that can be tapped into, rather than opting for sole dependence on a national grid.

The integral-ecological perspective of the Akashic Age, supported by the science behind nonlocal consciousness, could help in shifting our collective intelligence toward reflecting on integrating our lifestyles within our environments. No real change can be achieved without a corresponding change in consciousness.

Another natural energy source that is, quite literally, right beneath our feet is geothermal energy. And if a disaster, such as an earthquake or an explosion, occurred at a geothermal plant, the worst effect would be the need to rebuild it—little else. Our natural world has given us a huge abundance of energy sources that ebb and flow within the context of our everyday environment. Dramatic increases in commercial and local investments in such projects are crucial.

A more midrange energy resource could well be magnetic power, which has already been developed to some degree in recent years. It could turn out that the power of magnetism will become a major player at the dawn of the Akashic Age. The problem with energy is that a large percentage of it goes into overcoming friction, causing much of the power to be wasted, rather than utilized. Magnetism, as a power source, would permanently reduce energy use as well as energy waste and pollution. Examples of the use of this today are magnetic levitating trains (maglev) that hover above a set of rails containing magnets. Countries leading the way in this technology are Japan, Germany, and China. Already maglev trains have established world records, such as the MLX01 maglev train in Japan that set a speed record of 361 mph in 2003.

A longer-term, somewhat controversial, form of future energy could come from fusion power. There are currently many grand, expensive fusion projects under way. However, because of the huge amount of money required to bring them to fruition, they remain under direct government control. The European Fusion Development Agreement (EFDA), an agreement between European fusion research institutions and the European Commission, aims to demonstrate that nuclear fusion is a viable, long-term, safe, and environmentally benign future energy option. The EFDA currently funds the Joint European Torus (JET), which is Europe's largest fusion device.

The central question may not only concern our future energy sources, but specifically how such alternative energy can be efficiently utilized for a diverse planetary society. As we have previously noted, we feel that the answer to this question will come from the development and growth of distributed, networked infrastructures that will bring people into a more local and collaborative relationship with the sources and flows of available energy.

DISTRIBUTED ENERGY NETWORKS

The revolution in information communications has not only reconfigured how to share, distribute, and utilize networks of connectivity but has also "rewired" much of our current thinking. In terms of dealing with flows of information/energy, we are now able to envision a distributed model whereby electricity is generated from many smaller, more localized energy sources. Distributed energy networks allow energy to be produced and collected from many sources, thereby lowering environmental impacts and fostering greater self-sufficiency. It is a model that, like the Internet, can be built to withstand shocks, attacks, and breakages. When one line is cut, we can reroute and reconnect at a later point in the network. This decentralized model offers greater individualization—a diversity of interactions—within a shared, wide-ranging network. It would be possible to utilize it to configure our flows of energy in the near term.

We lose a great deal of our energy in transmission when delivering it over great distances. It has been noted that 98 percent of power failures originate in the distribution grid.[7] When the source is close to the users, we end up with a more reliable and cost-effective energy system. This suggests a growth in smaller power generators, located closer to the users. This would prompt many communities to develop their own forms of energy production to provide for their needs. Individuals would be encouraged to source their own energy requirements from a combination of solar, wind, and geothermal alternatives, with the option to sell back surplus energy into the national grid. This system of selling back surplus energy could be further associated with regional authorities, offering generous subsidies for families to invest in it.

This type of thinking aligns us closer to the reality of renewable energies that, by their very nature, are distributed throughout the planet in greater or lesser amounts. It would support the emergence of smaller scale, distributed energy production that could harness and store power locally.

The coming revolutions in energy could begin to gain ground by utilizing Internet technology to transform our (inter)national power grids into a distributive and integrated "smart grid," whereby millions of individual locations become local energy generators. Over the next decade, we can expect to see energy companies investing heavily in smart-grid technology and the early rollout of a new energy architecture, to allow power to flow in both directions. This model would be flexible enough to respond to changing consumer needs.

These developments could lead to the next generation of smart-grid networks, where connected devices would monitor and communicate their power usage and status, thus increasing efficiency. The system could rely on digital technologies in order to handle input and distribution from upwards of tens of thousands of local energy producers. The nature of local energy production would be transformed.

The coming years are crucial if we are to focus on developing a "green-architecture" model. Buildings themselves would become mini–power plants, harvesting energy from solar panels, windows, heat distribution, and a whole array of other strategies for tapping naturally produced energy. Dwellings can become dual-purpose, serving as living habitats as well as on-site energy generators. In this way we do not necessarily have to rely on constructing a whole new network of local energy generators—we can transform our existing buildings into energy sources, rather than using them as energy sinks.

By converting our energy sinks into energy sources, we will be revolutionizing not only the way energy is captured and stored, but also its location and distribution. This shift in the geography of energy production would go far toward democratizing the energy system and empowering millions of local users and communities. This can start happening within the current decade, as the transition in energy becomes a key to the dawn of the Akashic Age. However, huge investments will be needed by 2050, in order to transform our global energy system into a networked grid utilizing vast numbers of locally distributed energy producers. The concept of millions of separate local energy producers—small communities, individuals, and buildings, producing their own energy and selling it back into the grid—can inspire and empower developing countries as well.

As we mentioned previously, many developing countries could leapfrog directly into the emerging revolutionary model by adopting a smart grid that would connect thousands of energy producers. Many local, rural, stand-alone, decentralized, renewable power–generating hubs could share electricity across large regions. For example, Africa has nine times the solar potential of Europe, as well as a vast array of other natural resources, such as wind and hydroelectric. Also, Africa has hardly any existing energy infrastructure, so it could create a connected network of alternative energy production from the ground up. Through this model, Africa could easily supply its own needs and even export the surplus.

Due to the vast range of natural resources in such developing regions as Africa, India, China, and South America, strong growth and rapid change could take hold in these regions. Already there is a growing market for the lower-end scale of local energy generators, especially those utilizing solar power. In India, for example, electricity from solar is often cheaper than that from diesel generators. India's so-called "solar mission" is to install generators producing 20,000 megawatts of solar power by 2022. With increasing solar production coinciding with the ever-decreasing costs of solar technology, this potential for high growth in solar energy in developing countries could become a reality.

A vision for the Akashic Age could see this bottom-up, horizontal revolution emerging faster in developing countries, since many poor areas have a greater immediate need for it. Also, many such regions never experienced either a First or a Second Industrial Revolution, so there are few or no existing structures to take down or to transform. It would be like starting on a blank slate, enabling the renewable energy domain to rise at incredible speed. Many developing countries could find themselves at the forefront in fully utilizing their as-yet-underdeveloped renewable energy potential.

NEW EDUCATIONAL MODELS

Lifestyle priorities and commitments are a major part of the transition to an Akashic Age. Thus we will need to rethink the way we educate ourselves and the next generation.

Our present educational models are a remnant from the Industrial Era where children were educated to enter the workforce right from school. This has been updated nominally over the years, as students have become trained to be competitive and autonomous workers. Yet students are still expected to strictly obey authority figures, where sharing with others is seen as "cheating," and therefore a punishable offense. These educational models foster single-mindedness and self-centered competition, rather than nurturing, caring, and collaborative skills. Yet the world we are entering is a vastly more complex one than the Industrial Era, and the majority of educational institutions are ill equipped for the relations, interconnections, and communications that characterize it.

The old pedagogical model is not only increasingly out of touch with the current world but also, more importantly, out of sync with any vision of a positive future. What is taught across our school systems is in danger of becoming archaic overnight and limiting, or even harmful, to a younger generation of emerging creative minds. Furthermore, within the next decade there will be a projected global shortage of 18 million teachers worldwide, such as India, which needs another 1.2 million teachers, and also the United States, which will be lacking 2.3 million.[8] Our current system not only is increasingly unsuitable for our changing needs, it is also failing to give the next generations the tools they need for the future. We need to embrace the world that we're poised to enter, rather than training minds for a world that is on the way out.

As we outlined earlier, the new paradigms that emerge in science are rewriting our understanding of our place in the universe and highlight our inherent interconnectedness. We are fundamentally altering the very way we perceive human existence, and the potential for human evolution. Our new discoveries and understanding are developing faster than school text-books and curriculums can be rewritten. Our children are learning skills and adapting to the wider environment—perceiving events and issues more rapidly than our school systems are even able to realize. We need to undergo an educational paradigm shift in the years ahead, retooling how we approach learning. This could entail a dramatic move away from the enclosed class-room, surrounded by four brick walls, into a global space of learning.

For example, schools and universities will increasingly be linked up across the globe with students interacting and sharing their work and resources with peers from around the world. The classroom will become a lot more interactive and diverse, with students sharing projects with par-ticipants on different continents. Students will also rely more and more on their own peers to evaluate and comment on their work.

Schools, colleges, and universities will shift to become more online and thus more global and networked. Our educational institutions will make use of new software systems that not only facilitate students meet-ing in an online classroom, but also develop peer-assessment and feedback on their work. Learning and analyzing such issues as society and culture, sustainability, ecology, consciousness, new sciences, and the like will be so much more rewarding when students interact with other students from diverse backgrounds. Such learning environments will also help educa-tion break out of its strict academic specializations and embrace a more cross-disciplinary approach. Integrating fields of knowledge, rather than separating them, will promote a vision of the world as a planetary com-munity, nurturing diversity within unity.

This vision is not without support: the extension of our learning envi-ronments is already taking place, with such well-known higher education institutions as MIT agreeing to make available online their classes for free use and distribution. Likewise, the Khan Academy, created in 2006 by Salman Khan (a graduate of MIT and Harvard Business School), provides free, high-quality education to anyone, anywhere by means of an online collection of more than three thousand microlectures via video tutorials. Similarly, Academic Earth, a website launched in early 2009, offers a broad range of free online video lectures collected from major universities around the world.

In the fall of 2012, a world university has come online, dedicated to an educational system based on the new paradigm emerging in the sciences. The Giordano Bruno University aims to provide the scientific and humanistic concepts and insights that can empower young people and people young in spirit to evolve the new thinking and the new consciousness. The Giordano Bruno University aspires to provide information and knowledge on the basis of which people can develop the wisdom and the determination to become conscious architects of a more sustainable, equitable, and peaceful world.

An online repository of free resources, available direct to anyone with access to the Internet, will be a growing source of knowledge in the years ahead. By adopting and extending the social networking model, we can also create spaces for students, families, and teachers to come together—to ask questions, offer help, and connect with others studying related topics. Such online networks could help reshape the world's learning environment into one global study group.

Such a dramatic change in our educational environments could be instrumental in helping to break down physical, psychological, emotional, and mental barriers. Education would be moving out of the classroom, its once-restrictive cell, and into the wider human community. Students would be able to experience broader sociocultural contexts while practicing empathy, understanding, and tolerance. This model of distributed peer-to-peer learning shifts the focus from the lone individual to the wider, interdependent group. In this way the learning process ceases to be an isolated experience between an authority figure (the teacher) and a passive learner (the student). Not only is learning transformed into a community experience, but, importantly, the learner is encouraged to be an active participant in the learning process. This is markedly different from the old pedagogic model that expects students to absorb and regurgitate information.

Education in the years ahead could make a revolutionary shift toward the collaborative model. We will see students learning from networks of fellow students and resources, making the learning experience one of interaction and interplay. This new model is creative, fun, dynamic, and student centered. It incorporates online social networks and multicollaborations, and could also make use of online world-building games to develop strategic thinking. An educational model could emerge in the coming years, focused on personalized learning and open to anyone who has Internet access, regardless of time zone or location.

To summarize, the educational models of each era reflect, and teach, the defining consciousness of that era. Our current models reflect an outdated consciousness. As such, they are redundant in regard to the paradigm that is now emerging. We need to adjust our educational models to embrace the consciousness that reflects the Akashic Age we are moving into. As we have discussed, the latest discoveries in the new sciences tell us that the human self is entangled within the community of all living systems. Future learning models need to reflect the student's participation within the larger living system that is the biosphere. If we don't embrace these changes within our educational institutions, we risk alienating our younger generations, who are already rejecting the old modes of learning.

We can never go back from this point in time, as there is no world to go back to. It no longer exists—it has been transformed while we have been living in it. For the fish that swim in the river, the water is never the same; it is continually flowing. No fish ever swims in the same spot twice, unless it is within stagnant water. If our world stagnates—does not drive itself forward—then it will most likely collapse on itself. Our grand human-social-planetary-evolutionary project is too important for this to occur. It will not occur: we are already witnessing the emergence of young people who are effective change agents. They embody Mahatma Gandhi's advice in being the change they want to see in the world.

PART THREE

The Conscious Advent of the Akashic Age

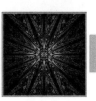

8

BUILDING THE WORLD
OF 2030

Now we take a big step: we go from vision to reality. Of course, the reality we go to is an anticipatory reality; the big step calls for a fast-forward from 2013 to 2030. Doing this is a useful exercise. It is an exercise not in utopian thinking, but in a realistic envisioning of the world we *could* build—if, that is, we took into consideration the problems as well as the opportunities, the bottlenecks as well as the resources, that confront the world after 2012.

The objectives outlined in this chapter are altogether realistic. They may sound idealistic or even utopian today, but they are only seen that way in the context of a stable, self-sustaining world. When the world in which we live is prone to breakdown, when it is moving toward a critical level of instability, the status quo is not an option. Even radical changes become realistic. This is the unique opportunity placed in our hands in the epoch that opens beyond 2012. In this epoch the world can change, adopting an Akashic Age worldview, because it *must* change. And it can change for the better, if the change is based on a conscious assessment of what needs to change—and also what could and should change.

The former—the vision for our future—was the topic of chapter 7. In this chapter we take up the latter task, making that vision a reality. We embark on the ambitious, but no longer utopian, exercise of describing the world we could build in the years now ahead of us.

THE POST-2012 EPOCH

In the disruptive years between 2012 and 2020, the world saw many systems coming apart as the strains and stresses of the economic-industrial model of perpetual growth could no longer be maintained.

The illusion of a world based on growth came rapidly undone in the public domain, as heavily debt-laden countries were forced to implement increasingly harsh and vastly unpopular austerity measures. Social protests, civil disobedience, and national strikes began to spring up almost everywhere in the world. Especially hard hit were the Western nations, as the shock of financial breakdown led to a sudden decrease in standards of living that most economies were unprepared for. The banking sector, in particular, became a direct target of people's frustration, as many Western nations finally admitted they were suffering through a prolonged depression, rather than a short-term recession. Job security was no longer guaranteed and the number of unemployed people rose sharply. The United States saw a dramatic increase in poverty, as millions became dependent on food stamps and other social-welfare programs. Online protests swelled and morphed into a mix of well-organized and intelligent protesting, as well as spontaneous, aggressive, and emotional rioting. Then the inevitable global economic collapse had finally occurred.

At the same time, many developing nations, particularly those based along the infamous Pacific Ring of Fire, suffered from increasing environmental, meteorological, and geological disturbances, ranging from earthquakes, tsunamis, tornados, and several high-level volcanic eruptions. In addition to high fatalities, these freak weather disruptions also contributed to huge numbers of climate migrants.

Countries in the Middle East and North Africa also fared poorly in these years, as unstable political regimes continued to use oppressive force to try to stem a rising tide of public anger and protest. Several regions erupted into civil war, exacerbated by opposition forces who received arms supplies from Western nations attempting to gain influence in the region. This happened most often in countries that were rich in natural resources.

Global communications allowed for all these events to be viewed across the world, on television, via Internet sites and mobile phones, and through a whole range of social media. Many people began to see through the official stories and realized that global instability, rather than being alleviated, was being perpetuated and exacerbated by official policy and interventionist strategies. This compounded the anger building against entrenched systems, and further alienated people from mainstream models. The Internet became a major arena—in fact, a global commons—for people to meet, share ideas and visions, and self-organize themselves into new networks and groups.

At first, many governments attempted to restrict Internet access through new laws that were allegedly designed to counter cybercrime and terrorist networks. Yet this subterfuge soon became transparent and a globally organized protest, launched by major organizations and well-respected individuals, rallied against the new laws and managed to overturn them.

However, global communications were not the only area of dissent. Due to civil unrest, many governments began to implement increasingly draconian and authoritative laws in order to maintain control. This turned into a clash of philosophies as the old consciousness of hierarchy, power, and ownership became heavily contested by the emerging consciousness of communication, cooperation, and collaboration.

Many intelligent networks and organizations were formed and began to come together to create new models to replace the old ones. Localization became a significant concept and many people began to develop vegetable gardens, create local currency and bartering systems, and start local energy production. Global communications were utilized to put local organizations in touch with one another, sharing information and skills. Urban development became a major focus of growth, as many people living in big cities were unable to relocate. Some governments introduced schemes to bring energy production into cities through modern, "green" architecture and energy-storing materials. Governmental leaders began to realize that they could not keep fighting against civil unrest.

From 2020 onwards, a new aspiration emerged, focused on public well-being and citizen participation. Technology became a stimulus for much urban planning and redevelopment. A new phase in alternative energy production and use became the centerpiece of global economic growth.

The decade leading up to 2030 was fraught with difficulties, struggle, and uncertainty; yet great change was ushered in. In this decade, new models, new ways of doing things, and collaborative relations succeeded in phasing out the ways of doing things that had prevailed since the Industrial Revolution. The consciousness that dominated the world in the twentieth century was replaced by a new consciousness—a consciousness of the inherent oneness of our species and its emerging global civilization. Although society was by no means perfect, nor was life free of problems, by 2030 a stable planetary society has started to emerge.

FAST-FORWARD: THE WORLD AT 2030

The World We Could Create, Told As If
We Had Created It

Dateline 2030

In the year 2030, the world enjoys a significant measure of unity within its diversity: nations that were once enemies and then became trading partners are now allies in creating and developing a peaceful global society.

The New Worldview

The fears that dominated the first decade of this century—fears of terrorism, armed conflict, economic breakdown, famine, and ecological collapse have been left behind. Stability is the hallmark of the 2030 world. This is not the rigid stability imposed by a powerful authority, but the stability of a sustainable network of self-reliant but cooperative communities, states, nations, and federations of nations.

Even if there is a diversity of worldviews on the five continents, there is a common element underlying them: humanity is seen as a diverse yet unified species, embedded in the cosmic sea of energy and information that connects all things in space and time. People are part of a new era of communication, collaboration, and connectivity; this manifests as an empathic, evolutionary, and integral consciousness. The new consciousness is inspired by discoveries in the sciences (quantum physics, cosmology, nanotechnology, evolutionary biology, neuroscience, and others), all of which reinforce the connected view of human beings and their interconnectedness within the larger community of living systems. This worldview has birthed the Akashic consciousness that embraces the entire human family.

The worldview that orients life in 2030 is not the same kind of view that prevailed at the turn of the millennium. People's thinking has changed, not by rules and legislation and fear of punishment, but by adopting new notions about the nature of the world, and by evolving a new consciousness.

The fundamental aspiration is inner rather than outer growth—the growth of social, intellectual, spiritual, and emotional life. Held in esteem are those who have integrity and sound ethics; who contribute to a better life for family, community, and humanity; who safeguard the balances and processes of nature; and who seek to discover deeper insight into the meaning of life.

Personal achievement used to be measured by the amount of money people had and the power they wielded. This is not the case any longer. The possession of wealth is not the measure of personal achievement, and material goods are not its outer sign. The symbol of social status is not a bigger home and car, and the mark of success is not the yacht and the private jet. Being rich is defined not by *having,* but by *being.*

Possessing material goods beyond what's needed to ensure a decent quality of life is not a sign of achievement; on the contrary, it's an indication of backward thinking. Living well means living wisely and comfortably; yet wealth is not measured by the quantity of goods one owns and controls, but by the quality of one's living experience. Real wealth lies in living a fulfilling life, with loving families, healthy and happy children, a caring community, and a healthy environment.

Patterns of Living

Urban planning has created cities that are favorable to easy mobility and navigation. Instead of having segregated areas, many of the larger cities have been redesigned to be functionally integrated between living, working, and leisure areas. Community living has become more integrated as people with different skill sets are close by, rather than living apart in accordance with their economic status, as in the past. This is because many urban areas make use of local barter economies so that a wide variety of skill sets are now more important than traditional income status.

Public spaces have been transformed into integrated and interconnected walkable networks and easy-access corridors. A revitalized sense of community infuses many cities, as open spaces, parks, community landscaping projects, community gardens, and food gardens have proliferated. Urban dwellers flock to local shopping areas and farmers' markets. Many of the old mega–shopping complexes have been transformed into community centers where people meet to network and organize local sustainable projects. People invest in community bonding, networks of friendship and well-being. The old days of debt-ridden consumerism fell by the wayside when the global financial markets collapsed. The ethic now is to live comfortably within one's means so that others can live comfortably as well.

Many towns have become walkable, pedestrian-friendly communities and have banned the use of individual transport. Transportation within towns and cities is supplied by public transport. Major cities have constructed trams and monorails to serve their aboveground areas. The majority of aboveground transport is driverless, powered by magnetism. Smaller towns have either trams or electric-battery-powered buses. Individual transport—that is, the motor vehicle—is restricted to rural and medium-distance travel. Cars are battery-powered and have strict quotas of energy consumption.

The living areas, whether urban or rural, work toward maximizing human interaction. The emphasis is on the recycling of goods and waste, efficient alternative energy production, and localized distribution. Each community supports its citizens through training courses, events, tools and techniques, resources, and emotional well-being support groups.

Communities throughout the world are connected with each other via global communications and have established a vast range of practical initiatives that support each other in ways that make life more harmonious, fulfilling, and equitable than ever before. Projects and schemes around the world make food production once again a prime aspect of family and civic life, including gardening workshops for growing your own food. There is public assistance for "self-farmers." Neighborhoods are sourcing water supplies and introducing local permaculture schemes. Social networks seek to bring home gardeners together to share tips, advice, and friendship. Many networks of investors, donors, entrepreneurs, and farmers exist, committed to building local food systems and local economies. Information is shared between regional, national, and international networks. In many rural regions, a form of eco-communalism has emerged that promotes localism, diversity, and autonomy, and is guided by the small-is-beautiful philosophy.

Several medium-size cities have redesigned themselves along the "garden-cities" concept popularized in the twentieth century. These cities are merging rural partnerships with urban dynamics, and constitute built-up living and working areas surrounded by agricultural land, green belts, and public spaces. The garden-city concept has become popular and is an inspiration for communities wishing to accommodate increased agricultural spaces for growing vegetables. Garden cities also engage in permaculture as a way of combining sustainable living zones with agricultural systems. Permaculture has become an established way of integrating the ecology of natural agricultural practices with the needs of the community.

Demographics

People live longer and healthier lives, but the world's population is not increasing. Longer life spans are offset by smaller families: many people realize that it is irresponsible to produce more children than one can care for. Also, since well-being is central to life, and essential services are provided—such as access to goods, services, transportation, information, education, health care, communication, human rights, democratic institutions—there is no need for large families.

A more equitable standard of living has negated the need for large families, as security and well-being are guaranteed. As a result, world population has stabilized around 7.5 billion. Compared to 2020, many countries in Asia and Africa have a tenfold increase in well-being, have one-half fewer babies, and live thirty years longer. Poverty has been reduced more in the past decade than in the previous five centuries. This brings many benefits. With a modest family size, people are able to take better care of their children, ensuring that they grow into healthy individuals, with sufficient education to live peacefully and sustainably.

Education

The systems of education have changed. Learning is not segmented into individual compartments and disciplines, but rather is transdisciplinary. While the specific features vary from community to community and region to region, the curricula of schools and universities have elements in common. Their basic mission is to educate a generation of locally active and globally thinking planetary citizens, able to live a healthy, productive, and responsible life, in harmony with each other and with nature.

Educational centers—schools, colleges, and universities—are linked up globally and promote student interaction and the sharing of resources. Classes are available online for those who are not able to attend physically, or who wish to revisit the courses.

Students are encouraged to create projects together with other students in other parts of the globe. Often, teachers serve at many different schools and universities. They offer their services to many institutions, interacting, teaching—and learning from—students from all cultures.

The new model of learning has shifted the focus from the individual learner to the learning, exploring group. Learning has ceased to be an isolated experience, limited to interaction between an authority figure and students; it has morphed into a shared experience. This model of collaborative learning has stimulated students to extend their sense of self and promote their participation in many different learning and living communities.

Before the transitional years, people thought that empathy, intuition, and spontaneous insight were esoteric concepts. They were surprised when more and more children were born with a capacity for them. These children were at first called "indigo children," but, as time passed, the new mental capacities became the norm, rather than the exception, and terms such as *indigo* and *new age* vanished from the vocabulary.

Politics

The recognition of humanity's connectedness within the web of life has given birth to a new political orientation. The states, nations, and federations are free to choose their preferred social structures and domestic systems. This doesn't prompt irremediable conflict. The human community has not been fragmented into isolated units, pursuing separate goals without regard for the common good. Rather, the many diverse nations and cultures are united by common values and aspirations, centered on creating a world where all people can live safely and peacefully without destroying each other and their life-sustaining environment.

The regional blocs that marked the political landscape at the beginning of the twenty-first century have been consolidated into four continental federations: European Union (EU), American Union (AMU), Pacific Union (PU), and African Union (AU). Within these federations, many lesser unions coordinate national policies and projects. Not only did warfare become too expensive, but it also became unnecessary as the world switched predominantly to renewable energies and resources. A global infrastructure of smart grids regulates a myriad of localized energy production at the source. Many of the deserts of North Africa are now the solar heart of Europe, whereas China's deserts supply solar energy to the Pacific Union.

Multiple networks of cooperation crisscross the interlinked social, political, and economic spheres. Individuals jointly shape and develop their local communities. These communities participate in broader collaborative networks that include, but do not stop at, the level of nations. Nation-states, in turn, are part of continental social and economic federations. Within these federations, smaller-scale unions help to coordinate the local and the continental institutions. Civil society has become an increasingly important area of life, as people are empowered to participate directly in both local and continental affairs, and even in global decision making.

Global forums decide questions of peace and security, the protection of the environment, information and communication, and international finance. The principal forum at this level is the United Peoples' Council, the body that succeeded the United Nations. The UPC observes, as do all other decision-making organs, the well-known but previously seldom-respected "principle of subsidiarity": decisions are to be made at the lowest level at which they can be effective. The global level of the UPC, the world's highest level of decision making, is at the same time the lowest level at which peace and security can be effectively safeguarded, the world environment can be cared for, and the flow of finance, technology, and information across the continents can be regulated. All other issues of public policy are delegated to local communities, to nation-states, and to the regional federations.

The UPC's political members are formed from the continental federations. The federations jointly constitute the Peacekeeping Council of the UPC, holding a mandate similar to that of the former Security Council, but without the two-tier structure where some members are permanent and others are not, and some have veto power and others do not. The Peacekeeping Council commands the sole significant military force in the world: the United Peacekeeping Force (UPF). The UPF, staffed by contingents from the continental federations, undertakes peacekeeping missions at the request of the UPC, in consultation with the federation where the mission is to be carried out.

The United Peoples' Council is not only a political organization: it has members from civil society and from business. Civil society members include federations of the many thousands—according to some estimates more than a million—nongovernmental organizations active in the social, economic, and environmental domains. Through their representation in the UPC, NGOs have become an integral part of the deliberations that decide the sustainability, the fairness, and the responsible development of local communities.

In tandem with the UPC's civil-society membership, the corporate membership is made up of federations of businesses in the major branches of industry. Through specialized agencies in finance, manufacturing, commerce, and labor, inherited from the United Nations and reformed in light of the council's enlarged mandate, the UPC connects its member business federations with representatives of the communities in which they operate. It helps managers establish good community relations, create mutually agreed-upon codes of conduct, and reach mutually beneficial agreements on technology transfer, trade, employment, finance, and protection of the environment.

Global-level coordination is a precondition of successfully restoring the viability of the environment: reestablishing natural balances in the composition of air, water, and soil, and preserving the integrity of the biosphere's regenerative cycles. In view of this requirement, the World Environment Organization has been created as a global-level partner of the United Peoples' Council, with the mandate to coordinate the environmental programs of the regional federations. It works closely with the political, the business, and the civil-society members of the UPC.

The continental and subcontinental level is effective for coordinating decision making at the level of nation-states. The regional federations provide a forum for the representatives of their member nations to discuss their concerns, explore areas of mutual interest, and coordinate their political goals and socioeconomic practices.

The tasks and responsibilities of nation-states have not changed significantly. National governments remain the principal arbiters of their country's economic and social imperatives. The states maintain a national economic body, a national judicial system, a police force, and a health care system. But national institutions do not operate under the premise of absolute sovereignty. Domestically, they are integrated with the administrations of cities and rural areas, and internationally with the states that share a given regional federation.

Although political parties still exist, there are many independent politicians who stand apart from the platform of a particular party. Some nations have opted for leaders who answer directly to the people, rather than as representatives of political parties.

The local level of coordination and decision making serves cities, towns, and villages. At this community level, direct democracy is the rule: the representatives of the people respond directly to the people. The customary mechanism is the town hall meeting, held face-to-face whenever and wherever possible, and electronically when distance or cost prevents a significant number of people from participating in person.

Governments are not formed exclusively of politicians; they include representatives from all walks of life, including civil society, community representatives, trade representatives, scientists, well-known thinkers/intellectuals, architects/designers, and artists.

Business is no longer a separate "private" sector; companies have become a functional part of the host communities. As some corporate leaders did in the last part of the twentieth century, managers endeavor to overcome the tension between efficiency, profitability, and dynamism on the one hand, and solidarity, equity, and sustainability on the other. They select the products and services they bring to the market in consultation with their clients and customers, and their employees and partners. Business responsibility to the community and to customers is a mainstay of business practice. Production and marketing decisions are made not only with an eye toward success in the marketplace but also in view of minimizing impact on the environment, achieving employee satisfaction, and maximizing human and social usefulness. The principal aspiration is not merely to increase value for the shareholders, but to promote social and ecological responsibility for all stakeholders.

Finance

The financial system has been thoroughly redesigned. The UPC issues a world credit currency, the Gaia, on the basis of the human, and not the financial, capital of a federation—that is, the size of its population, not the size of its treasury. The federations have their own forms of credit, which they put into circulation and take back through taxes. These national credits are used for trade between the federations' member states; the Gaia is reserved for interfederation transactions.

There is a whole array of complementary local and regional credits in use for health services, education, social welfare, energy, and culture. These digital credits are earned and swapped through global Internet networks. Electronic payments are the norm throughout the world. The idea of using paper or metal currency is considered archaic. Some of the credits in circulation can be earned in the form of an energy swap, whereby local energy producers send back surplus energy into domestic grids. Other credits are earned from various forms of community work, civil service, national and/or international volunteer work, and all forms of regular employment. Through the use of such currencies, even the least developed economies have overcome marginalization and dependence on industrialized economies and global financial institutions.

The diversified yet interlinked monetary system, based on the trading function of digital credits, rather than on its ability to earn interest, ensures that global wealth does not accrue to an ever-smaller minority. It does away with profit-motivated speculative bubbles and the inflation of national currencies. It is an effective mechanism for buffering financial crises and redressing instabilities in the international economy.

9

THE PILLARS OF A NEW CONSCIOUSNESS

The younger generations are emerging rapidly, with sharp and insightful patterns of thinking. They are aware of the changes occurring on the planet: they are born into a world in transformation. They arrived already hardwired for change. Over the next few decades this hyperaware generation will grow, develop, and eventually seed the transformational change on the planet. This change will usher in a new society—a society that may be incomprehensible to the older generation. That is why we call the new generation the Phoenix Generation: it will rise from the ashes of the old systems.

THE PHOENIX GENERATION: A GENERATION WAKING UP

More and more reports from educators, therapists, and social workers reveal the radically different nature of the new generation. Dr. Linda Silverman, a clinical and counseling psychologist who runs the Gifted Development Center in Colorado (United States), has studied gifted children for over forty-five years. She writes:

> I have been astonished by the children who have come into my life in recent years. It feels like they are a new breed . . . Their heredity

and environment are not fundamentally different from all the children we've encountered in the past. Yet, there is a remarkable difference in these children from the children we've known in the past. The only explanation I can think of is evolution. I believe we are witnessing the evolution of the human species . . .[1]

Psychologist Kenneth Ring uses the word *edglings* to describe youngsters who seem to be closer to having achieved a high development in human potential than most of their peers. He likens these youngsters to individuals who have undergone sacred rituals that develop a spiritual sensitivity and a sense of the sacredness of the Earth. Similarly, social historians William Strauss and Neil Howe note a distinct characteristic of the new generations of young people. Many of them display a temperament that manifests civic-mindedness, optimism, fierce independence, a sense of purpose, and a centered form of personal energy.[2]

It is becoming increasingly apparent that the younger generation is exhibiting a new form of consciousness, a new set of attitudes, and novel views of the world. While many in the older generations grew up trusting and abiding by authority without questioning that authority, members of the younger generation find themselves at odds with the current system. To them it seems irrational. For example, Julie Rosenshein, a psychotherapist and school consultant, notes that many children are not so much inattentive as they are selectively attentive.[3] When the classroom forces them into activities they consider meaningless or unimportant, they reject, refuse to pay attention, or revolt and lash out. The problem is that many of these children are constrained to act within the structures of old-paradigm education and parenting. Conventional schools aim to keep such children under control, rather than educating them and nurturing their creativity. The result is that many children are said to suffer from disorders, such as oppositional defiant disorder—a linear, old-paradigm category.

Members of the younger generation exhibit the new consciousness and, as adults, seek flexibility in the workplace, and an atmosphere that fosters creativity. They dress casually, and work in brightly colored

environments. They express and nurture a shared network of camarade-
rie. For such people, satisfaction in the workplace is a must.

Bruce Doyle III, a business executive and consultant, sees the new
wave of young adults as wanting to work for people who respect them, in
a place that permits self-expression. They are not concerned with stereo-
types, or with having to adhere to fixed roles, and they especially rebel
against the orthodox judgments of others. Noticing these characteristics
in young employees, Doyle decided to do his own survey.[4] What he found
is that these young people have a strong passion for self-expression, for
helping others, for achieving life goals, and for engaging in loving relationships. For example, when asked, "What are you committed to in
your life?" the largest response category (57 percent) came up with replies
such as "Changing the 'systems' to help people in crisis"; "Championing
issues concerned with quality of life, as opposed to a focus on quantity
of life"; and "Giving back to others and being a role model for children."
They also expressed strong personal values, such as being true to oneself,
freedom and independence, trust, honesty, respect, empathy, and loyalty.
They attached less importance to material values and possessions, and
more to achieving something of value in their lives.

Many of these young people are now entering professional social roles.
The wave of new thinking is creeping into the social infrastructure. It
will be from there, from within, that constructive change will come in
the coming years.

The dawn of the Akashic Age will herald the beginning of an era
when the human species begins to manifest a new form of consciousness: an integrated consciousness that does not tolerate the old paradigm
of ego-driven greed and materialism. A tidal wave of transformational
change will then sweep into society as a new generation itself becomes
the change.

MANIFESTO OF A NEW CONSCIOUSNESS

This Manifesto of a New Consciousness suggests the guiding values and
principles humanity needs to live and thrive on this planet. It is presented

here with the aim of generating further reflection and discussion on these values and principles—in everyone's urgent self-interest.

- I am part of the world. The world is not outside of me, and I am not outside of the world. The world is in me, and I am in the world.

- I am part of nature, and nature is part of me. I am what I am in my communication and communion with all living things. I am an irreducible and coherent whole with the web of life on the planet.

- I am part of society, and society is part of me. I am what I am in my communication and communion with my fellow humans. I am an irreducible and coherent whole with the community of humans on the planet.

- I am more than a skin-and-bones material organism: my body, and its cells and organs, are manifestations of what is truly me: a self-sustaining, self-evolving, dynamic system arising, persisting, and evolving in interaction with everything around me.

- I am one of the highest, most evolved manifestations of the drive toward coherence and wholeness in the universe. All systems drive toward coherence and wholeness in interaction with all other systems, and my essence is this cosmic drive. It is the same essence, the same spirit that is inherent in all the things that arise and evolve in nature, whether on this planet or elsewhere in the infinite reaches of space and time.

- There are no absolute boundaries and divisions in this world, only transition points where one set of relations yields prevalence to another. In me, in this self-maintaining and self-evolving coherence- and wholeness-oriented system, the relations that integrate the cells and organs of my body are prevalent. Beyond my body, other relations gain prominence, especially those that drive toward coherence and wholeness in society and in nature.

- The separate identity I attach to other humans and other things is but a convenient convention that facilitates my interaction with them. My family and my community are just as much "me" as the organs of my body. My body and mind, my family and my community, interact with and interpenetrate each other, variously prevalent elements in the network of relations that encompasses all things in nature and the human world.

- The whole gamut of concepts and ideas that separates my identity, or the identity of any person or community, from the identity of other persons and communities are manifestations of this convenient but arbitrary convention. There are only gradients distinguishing individuals from each other and from their environment and no real divisions and boundaries. There are no "others" in the world: we are all living systems and we are all part of each other.

- Attempting to maintain the system I know as "me" through ruthless competition with the system I know as "you" is a grave mistake: it could damage the integrity of the embracing whole that frames both your life and mine. I cannot preserve my own life and wholeness by damaging that whole, even if damaging a part of it seems to bring me short-term advantage. When I harm you, or anyone else around me, I harm myself.

- Collaboration, not competition, is the road to the wholeness that marks healthy systems in the world. Collaboration calls for empathy and solidarity, and, ultimately, for love. I do not and cannot love myself if I do not love you and others around me: we are part of the same whole and so are part of each other.

- The idea of *self-defense,* even of *national defense,* needs to be rethought. Patriotism, if it aims to eliminate adversaries by force, and heroism, even in the well-meaning execution of that aim, are mistaken aspirations. Patriots or heroes who brandish swords or guns are also enemies to themselves. Every weapon intended to hurt or kill is a danger to all. Comprehension, conciliation, and forgiveness are not signs of weakness; they are signs of courage.

- The "good" for me and for every person in the world is not the possession and accumulation of personal wealth. Wealth, in money or in any material resource, is but a means of maintaining myself in my environment. As exclusively mine, it commandeers part of the resources that all things need to share if they are to live and to thrive.

Exclusive wealth is a threat to all people in the human community. And because I am a part of this community, in the final analysis it is also a threat to me, and to all who hold it.

- Beyond the sacred whole that we recognize as the world in its totality, only life and its development have what philosophers call intrinsic value; all other things have merely instrumental value—value insofar as they add to or enhance intrinsic value. Material things in the world, and the energies and substances they harbor or generate, have value only if and insofar as they contribute to life and well-being in the web of life on this Earth.

- The true measure of my accomplishment and excellence is my readiness to give. The amount of what I give is not the measure of my accomplishment. Rather, the measure of my accomplishment is the relationship between what I give, and what my family and I need to live and to thrive.

- Every healthy person takes pleasure in giving: it is a higher pleasure than having. I am healthy and whole when I value giving over having. A community that values giving over having is a community of healthy people, oriented toward thriving through empathy, solidarity, and love among its members. Sharing enhances the community of life, while possessing and accumulating creates demarcation, invites competition, and fuels envy. The share-society is the norm for all the communities of life on the planet; the have-society is typical only of modern-day humanity, and it is an aberration.

PART FOUR

From Vision to Reality

Contributions from the
World-Shifting Community

A New Human . . . and a New World

JOHN L. PETERSEN

John L. Petersen is a futurist and strategist. He founded the Arlington Institute more than twenty years ago and is the editor and publisher of the internationally acclaimed e-newsletter, FUTUREdition. Petersen has written three books about different aspects of thinking about and influencing the future. He lives in Berkeley Springs, West Virginia, near Washington, D.C.

■ ■ ■

It's hard to anticipate the amount of damage that a storm will do before it is even on the horizon or, if you prefer, to handicap how well a marriage will work before the principals have even finished the entrée of their first dinner date. Big, significant events have always had the potential and propensity to write history in ways that didn't seem likely—or even possible—when considered before the fact.

This notion escalates proportionally: when the event gets bigger or comes faster, the uncertainty similarly increases. Wonderful serendipity may emerge, or not. And the postmortem will always contain surprises.

So how do you consider what a complex world might look like in 2020, after the most significant and far-reaching transitional shift in human history has disrupted and upended everything that came before? Well, it depends, of course, on what happens, but there *are* ways to systematically think about the alternatives, which could give us some indication not only of how we might prepare but also of how the outcome might be shaped.

Let's presume for the moment that the many ancient and esoteric sources that discuss this event are correct and this shift will do nothing less than prepare and present the planet for the emergence of a new world that operates in a radically new way. The heralds are different, but there are common themes: a new experience of oneness and interdependency, one thousand years of peace, extraordinary leaps in consciousness, and the emergence of a new multidimensional human reality, among others.

It's getting there that can kill you, they say, so we should think here a bit about how that new world might emerge and use those cues to navigate our way to this coming future.

ALTERNATIVE TRANSITION FUTURES

Our ability to effectively respond to great change varies, in part, with the degree of disruption we experience. The greater and more unfamiliar that disruption is, the harder it is for us to reorient, repair, and reconfigure things. There is a spectrum of disruption characterizations we can consider that is anchored on one end by Great Disruption and on the other by, let's call it, Rapid Evolutionary Change (if it was just evolutionary change, by definition, it wouldn't be particularly disruptive, and what seems to be on the way is some form of disruption). The Great Disruption has all kind of potential problems associated with it: earthquakes and volcanoes, failure of the global financial system, collapse of the planet's magnetosphere, big solar flares, rather rapid arrival of a mini–Ice Age, big energy explosions from the center of the galaxy—stuff like that. In this situation, you'd probably have failures of some of the energy and communications infrastructure, for example.

The Rapid Evolutionary Change alternative presupposes that there is disruption—maybe a series of financial crises, less rapid climate change, lesser solar activity, and the like. Still unusual and disruptive, but not so acute. And let's say that in this world there are no significant infrastructure failures.

Now, consider another spectrum of possibilities—how humans adapt to the transition. On this line, one end is defined by Hard and Rough, signifying a very tough adaptive response, and on the other end humans do better. It's not a piece of cake necessarily, but the disruptions bring out the best in us all and we reach new heights and become better people in the process. Let's call that Enlightened Engagement.

If you array these two spectrums orthogonally, you have something that looks like the diagram on page 120.

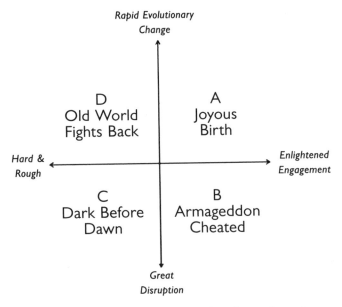

The arrayed spectrums of Hard and Rough and
Enlightened Engagement

These axes present the options of four different combinations of potential futures. By immersing ourselves in each of these possibilities, we can start to build a systems view of the options available to us.

Future A: Enlightened Engagement to Rapid Evolutionary Change

In this world we are experiencing rapid but not debilitating change and the supporting energy and communications infrastructures largely work. It is disruptive because even if it is largely defined by amazing new break-throughs in human and technological capabilities, these new gifts and tools will necessarily threaten the status quo and drive rapid and some-times destabilizing change into the existing economic, energy, governmental, and social systems, among others.

What this transition does suggest is that there are no great, rapid sys-tem failures—financial, energy, political, and the like—but rather that in some way (and there are a variety of theories about how that might happen), either through the emergence of new organizations and ideas or new human capabilities—or, more likely, a combination of the two—it becomes obvious that the old approach to doing things is not working and through elections, breakthroughs, campaigns, innovation, and other catalytic methods, the systems morph into new forms with new functions. Old things go away and things become new.

The change could be driven by the activation of portions of DNA that enable new human capabilities, new power-generation capabilities, climate change, Net-based new social communications tools, and perhaps rapid shifts in geopolitics in places like the Middle East.

This world—let's call it *Joyous Birth*—is defined by humanity effectively adapting to this disruptive but evolutionary change. Like childbirth, this does not mean that it is smooth or painless, but that it is manageable and, in the process, humanity rises to the occasion and a new world is born, populated by "new humans" who define themselves in significantly new ways.

Future B: Enlightened Engagement to Great Disruption

This is an interesting world where chaos is part of the equation. Abrupt change and failure, whether related to Earth changes (climate, earthquakes, volcanoes, tsunamis), unusual solar activity, human systems (financial, political, etc.), magnetosphere collapse and reorganization, physical pole shift, and technological breakthroughs (think WikiLeaks and new, revolutionary energy capabilities, for example) combine to put large elements of familiar human systems, processes, and perspectives in play. The energy and communications infrastructures continue to work, but there are a lot of moving pieces and some balls that don't stay in the air.

You'd think that the human response to all this upheaval would initially be similarly chaotic, fragmented, and ineffective, but in this world we all cope in some marvelous way. There may well be conventional approaches that allow humans to be agile, adaptive, and resilient enough in this context, but the easiest way to make sense of this possibility is through some extraordinary input or game reset.

There's always the extraterrestrial possibility, of course. Extraterrestrials show up, do tricks, tell us new things, and we all (or most of us, at least) shift to a new way of thinking and acting. Perhaps aberrant solar activity activates new levels of consciousness—opens us up to the fourth dimension and, rather suddenly, a new way of dealing with the old world becomes available. A number of indigenous groups reportedly believe something like this will happen and there are many new age (and historical) books that advance theories that would populate this space. Don't forget the Bible.

In any case, there is disaster all around, but somehow we are extricated/transformed/renewed so that we deal with the situation and build the new world. Sounds like *Armageddon Cheated* to me.

Future C: Hard and Rough Response to the Great Disruption

Everything hits the fan here and we have a hard time dealing with it. Here we need to be creative; without invoking magic, it might be possible to envision a situation where a large number of Earth changes worldwide happen sometime before the evolutionary jump takes place and we all participate in a degenerating old world for a time before the shift occurs. The implosion of present systems might be followed rapidly by extraordinary energy inventions and discoveries that would allow for rapid rebuilding. Perhaps this is another situation where we get help from new star friends who bring transformative ideas and tools. In any case, this world—I'll call it *Dark before Dawn*—drops us into a pretty deep hole that we find our way out of rather quickly.

Future D: Hard and Rough Response to Rapid Evolutionary Change

Here the change should otherwise be manageable but the transition turns out to be hard. Many (necessarily unconventional) sources suggest that a new world is absolutely going to evolve, but that we, humanity, are the ones who will decide how smooth the transition will be. The shift is sparked by solar cosmic energy, which initiates Earth changes and human genomic changes. Not everyone responds to the experience with love, compassion, gratitude, and a sense of interdependency and oneness, although enough do to ensure the ultimate arrival of the new world. Others find the shift a surprise at best and very disconcerting at worst, and do everything they can to sustain and maintain the familiar status quo—fighting against the flood of new perspectives and ideas. They lose, of course, but they struggle, hence the name, *The Old World Fights Back*.

WHAT TO DO?

The question now arises: How can we influence which world actually arrives? Some would suggest that we should spend a great deal of time and effort trying to think up new ways to do the big things that we now do, like government, finances, and economics—that we need new ideas that can replace the present ways things are done. But this new world by definition doesn't work on the same principles as our current one. It might be really strange.

So, what to do? We're dealing here with extraordinary, unprecedented change, which necessarily requires extraordinary, unprecedented intervention. So, we have to try something new. We have to participate in the evolutionary process and move ourselves into new thinking and new perspectives that approach the problem from a radically different angle—one that begins to mirror what we know about the operational behavior of the new world that is emerging. In a real sense, this is the big opportunity for us to begin to become—in a very practical way—new humans.

We are told that one of the characteristics of these new humans will be the ability to manifest things—using their minds to affect the physical world. That is, quite literally using consciousness to configure the fundamental energy from which everything emerges into specific outcomes. Essentially, it says that if you change your mind, you can change the world. Most of us believe that that is a lot easier said than done, but there is a fairly easy way to work your way into this space that has direct implications for the global futures that we all will experience.

The new human is about love—the fearless embracing of the whole of this human experience in an openhearted, inclusive way. It is about connecting with others and the rest of this world's creation with a transparency that is nurturing and compassionate, not fearful and destructive. Those feelings are a direct reflection of your operating frequency (we're all just energy, remember). The higher the frequency, the more open and light you feel.

These feelings do far more than just communicate a personal sense of good or bad—they condition the field around you. Your level of consciousness, which is reflected in the frequency that you project, reaches far out from your body and directly influences everything within range—people, plants, animals—everything. You literally influence everything you come in contact with.

Intention focuses consciousness. When you shape your intention around some mental image, your consciousness reaches out and begins to work on the underlying energy field to make it into the image you had in your mind. More than that, because your field of consciousness interacts with all those with whom you are in contact (and vice versa), if you get together with another person to imagine a similarly desired future, your commonly held vision becomes entrained around the same objective and, we are told, that entrainment is exponentially more powerful than if each of you envisioned that future separately.

So, if we can get enough people intending us toward the upper right-hand corner of our scenarios, we can literally influence both the amount of disruption and the way we respond to it in the coming years.

There are innumerable sources that clearly suggest that making common cause is important, but the typical initiatives of conventions, rallies, seminars, and celebrations seem to miss the essential nature of what needs to be accomplished here. The requirement is entrainment around a clear, rather explicit end. It is the notion of manifestation writ large—a dedicated group of like-minded people who gather together to visualize and intend and share the feelings of a new world that is defined in some degree of detail.

In a sense, what is needed is a common image—a picture—of some deeply representative experience in the new world. Perhaps we need to visualize a typical day, or an iconic experience, or a ceremony that weaves together the threads of the new human operating principles that are remembered and recited at a commonly experienced event, like the birth of a child. It would state who we are and how we, as new humans, are committed to living. It would be the collection of core, extensible principles, set in a structured context that can be graphically represented so as to present a common vision in the minds of the participating individuals.

If this vision were rendered creatively and effectively in both visual and narrative form, it could become an icon—a totem—that could be held up to represent the future that we desire. A symbol, like a logo, could be designed, one that would telegraph the essential message to all who saw it and understood its meaning.

The Internet is designed for this kind of initiative. Institutions are already organizing online meditations that circle the Earth twenty-four hours a day with participants in each time zone gathering together virtually to meditate on various themes at a particular time of day. Even a dedicated website that did nothing other than rerun a visual and narrative routine on the hour every hour in a variety of languages could provide a common touchstone for those who wanted to take part in such an imaging process.

Now is the time we should stand up for such an initiative. We are experiencing the first paradigm shift in the history of humanity where we, the major organism on the planet, have the capacity to both anticipate the kind of future that we would like and materially influence how it manifests. In the past, everyone just went along for the ride—they didn't know either what was happening to them or where they were going. Now it's different and we must rise to the occasion and play the role that we have evolved to play and actively shape the future coming our way.

THE OTHER SIDE OF THE SHIFT

NICOLYA CHRISTI

Nicolya Christi is a spiritual teacher and evolutionary guide for the times. Her latest book, *Contemporary Spirituality for an Evolving World: A Handbook for Conscious Evolution,* is slated for publication by Inner Traditions in September 2013. Christi is the founder of WorldShift Movement, cofounder of WorldShift International, and coinitiator of WorldShift 2012.

■ ■ ■

DECEMBER 21, 2012: THE GREAT SHIFT

For millions of people around the world, 2012 marked the pinnacle of an unprecedented human and global evolutionary shift.

Ancient prophecy foretold that the year 2012 would be a time when the old world would end and a new world would be born. Many past civilizations, especially, considered the date December 21, 2012, to be of great importance, including the ancient peoples of the Americas, Sumer, China, and Egypt.

The Qu'ero, direct descendents of the Incas, spoke of "An age of conquest and domination coming to an end and a new human being born." They called this process the "Turning of the Earth" and they identified 2012 as the time when this would unfold. The Hopi spoke of 12/21/12 as being the moment humanity enters "One thousand years of peace," and the Maya and other ancient indigenous peoples spoke of 12/21/12 as the threshold into "A New Golden Age."

The year 2012 also witnessed an extraordinary unfolding of rare cosmic events. Ancient prophecy appeared to be engaged in a sophisticated and synchronistic union of astronomical, astrological, and Great Calendar Completion Cycles. One example is the completion of the 5,126-year Mayan Long Count Calendar on 12/21/12—the same date as the completion of the 26,000-year Galactic Cycle.

126

A total solar eclipse occurred on August 11, 1999, at 11:11 a.m. Greenwich Mean Time (the same time as the 2012 winter solstice—11:11 a.m. Universal Time), which, according to Mayan prophecy, took humanity into a thirteen-year completion cycle that the Maya referred to as the Quickening.

The Maya foretold that these final thirteen years of the 5,126-year Long Count Calendar would be the last opportunity for our civilization to embrace the changes due to unfold at the moment of our collective spiritual regeneration in December 2012.

Millions across the globe could sense that something of an unprecedented nature was occurring during the time of the Quickening, and indeed throughout all of 2012. Millions of people around the world shared their extraordinary experiences of immense challenges and extraordinary potential via social media networks and related websites.

The date 12/21/12 marked the precise moment when important ancient prophecy and rare astronomical alignments converged, signaling a phenomenon unlike anything humanity had witnessed—the Great Shift.

Mayan messenger Carlos Barrios perfectly summed up the meaning of 2012:

The world will not end. It will be transformed. . . . Everything will change. . . . Change is accelerating now and it will continue to accelerate. If the people of the Earth can get to this 2012 date without having destroyed too much of the Earth, we will rise to a new, higher level. But to get there we must transform enormously powerful forces that seek to block the way.

Humanity will continue, but in a different way. Material structures will change. From this we will have the opportunity to be more human. Our planet can be renewed or ravaged. Now is the time to awaken and take action. The prophesied changes are going to happen, but our attitude and actions determine how harsh or mild they are.

This is a crucially important moment for humanity and for Earth. Each person is important. If you have incarnated into this era, you have spiritual work to do balancing the planet.

The greatest wisdom is in simplicity. Love, respect, tolerance, sharing, gratitude, forgiveness. It's not complex or elaborate. The real knowledge is free. It's encoded in your DNA. All you need is within you. Great teachers have said that from the beginning. Find your heart, and you will find your way.[1]

2013–2020:
THE OTHER SIDE OF THE SHIFT

So where do we find ourselves placed post–2012 Shift, in terms of our personal and collective evolutionary development? Let us now journey in our imaginations to visit the year 2020, as observers, and consider the following questions:

1. What do we notice about the inner-development process of the individual?
2. What tangible signs are there of individual and collective integration and evolution?
3. What has transpired in the eight years between 2013 and 2020 to reveal that world peace is a progressive and sustainable reality unfolding between people, communities, countries, and nations?
4. What new values and foundation stones are being set in place to ensure the establishment of sustainable world peace?

My own responses are as follows:

1. The evolution of consciousness has taken a progressive evolutionary leap forward. The awakened human in 2020 has embodied the authentic self, transcended the ego, is psychologically integrated and spiritually balanced. Such an individual understands not only the concept, but the living reality, that an inner shift is a prerequisite for a positive and lasting world shift, and how true inner peace creates lasting world peace.
2. Psychologically and spiritually balanced individuals have under-

gone a rapid phase of personal evolution. Thus, they qualify as cocreators and evolutionary guides for a new world paradigm. It is widely recognized that only those who have achieved an integrated balance, at a psychological and spiritual level, can successfully establish a positive, new, global, sociopolitical system.

3. The year 2020 holds a greater potential for world peace than at any other time. The millions of integrated individuals are the new evolutionary guides for humanity. They qualify to guide humanity into a new paradigm not merely because of their intellectual capacity, but, equally important, because they possess a highly refined emotional intelligence, and thus are able to develop and implement new holistic systems for all, including those between political authority and people.

What is clear from a 2020 vantage point is that not only are people tired of the old-paradigm models that keep government and people in duality, but governments, too, are tired of trying to stem the flow of a dysfunctional economic, ecological, sociological, and political system that runs deep in the fabric of society and that can never be resolved through old-paradigm governing patterns. Through new and global 2020 Advisory Councils, 2020 governing authorities are beginning to recognize that cooperation, collaboration, and co-creation with the people is the only way to ensure a win-win situation.

For millennia, humanity has endured extreme trauma, fundamentalism, war, conflict, dictatorship, uprisings, rebellion, cruelty, and revolution. We have been polarized in either fight or flight mentality and actions. Where is peace in the annals of our history?

There has never been a system of rule that has created a healthy economy that sustains us all. There has never been a unified political system that supports the needs and respects the rights of all. Despite the wealth of previous fallen empires, despite all the revolutions, protests, and campaigns, never has there been peace on earth, in the entire history of humankind.

The fact remains that, pre-2020, global authoritarians were not fully qualified to organize human society in ways that are crucial to human and global evolution.

We are mistaken or naive if we believe that most Western nations are living in peacetime. A war rages under our very noses and plays out in the political landscape and the media every day. It is an endless war that polarizes us in either fight or flight mode. We continue to remain unseen and unheard in any attempt to integrate an intelligent and sophisticated vision of collaboration with global authority systems.

Our human right to peace continues to elude us, even after millions and millions of deaths and casualties in the name of peace. It is blatantly obvious that many of the wars that cause untold human suffering and death are fought solely over resources and money. Even after wholesale tragedies—the people's removal of dictators who have decimated or ravaged entire countries, the unimaginable cruelty and torture that have been inflicted on our global brothers and sisters—we find that thousands of years later we are still experiencing the same entrenched patterns of duality governance* and heartbreaking realities of the abuse of people and planet for individual profit and national self-interest.

The stories of our ancestors and the consequences of their own fight for freedom have left a deep, traumatic imprint encoded in our DNA. If we are to transcend this traumatic pattern, we must establish conscious, intelligent, compassionate, and peaceful means in order to co-create together with existing global authority.

The need to integrate and heal the psychological split within ourselves and embrace a unified and harmonious political partnership is essential if we are ever to shift the balance and co-create with the systemwide sociopolitical systems in existence today. It will require psychologically integrated and spiritually balanced humanitarians to guide twenty-first-century humanity in a new direction. It is such people who can offer the greatest potential for the evolutionary transformation of humanity and a peaceful and sustainable global community.

---

*A governance that has a dualistic approach, that is, an "us verses them" mentality that polarizes and splits rather than unifies people.

4. The year 2020 holds promise of contemporary spirituality for an evolving world. As the psychological and conscious evolution of the individual and collective begins to establish a firm foothold as a reality, we find ourselves in the midst of a global spiritual evolution. Our relationship with spirituality is subject to radical questioning, as we sense the rumblings of change beneath the surface of the spiritual/religious ground we have stood upon for thousands of years.

As psychologically and consciously evolving individuals, we are now seeking and needing a more authentic expression of spirituality that speaks to who we are as consciously evolved twenty-first-century human beings. As the many layers that have hidden the heart of the true self are peeled away through psychological processing and conscious awakening, so too are we searching for an authentic spiritual and religious practice aligned with our evolving consciousness and the new-world paradigm that is emerging in alignment with the times.

We are now ready to strip away the layers that have hidden the heart of religion—layers designed to control and manipulate our ancestors who had not attained the degree of conscious evolution that is possible for us as twenty-first-century, awakened human beings.

Twenty-first-century humans seek a spiritual path to reflect the consciousness of the present times, one in which the heart of religion is laid bare. Our conscious evolution calls for a contemporary spiritual practice based solely on love—for it is love that is at the heart of all religions.

I have created these models as a response to how we may begin to establish a progressively conscious global society—an evolving global society that upholds new sociopolitical/spiritual ethics and promotes contemporary spirituality.

TEN FOUNDATION STONES OF
CONTEMPORARY SPIRITUALITY

- Unconditional Love
- Unconditional Positive Regard

- Compassion
- Empathy
- Understanding
- Transparency
- Mindfulness
- Equality
- Conscious Communication
- Unity Consciousness

SIX CORE VALUES FOR A
NEW PARADIGM

- Peace
- Restorative Justice
- Sustainability
- Compassionate Action
- Conscious Communication
- Conscious Evolution

TWELVE FOUNDATION STONES
FOR AN EVOLVING WORLD

- Equality
- Inclusivity
- Understanding
- Forgiveness
- Empathy
- Co-creation
- Cooperation
- Cosupport
- Collaboration
- Nonmonetary Transactions
- Nonviolent/Compassionate Communication
- Unconditional Giving, Receiving, and Doing

STEPPING OFF THE EDGE

The year 2012 took those of us who are psychologically and spiritually awake to the very edge of our evolutionary process in order to reveal the vast potential of all that lies beyond that point. The period leading to 2020 invites us to step off the edge of the old and into a new-world paradigm—one that urgently requires wise stewardship.

I conclude with a simple yet appropriate quote by Guillaume Apollinaire, which invites us to overcome historical programming that has us falsely believe that we may "fall" if we actively seek change, that our vision for humanity is "too high," and that the evolutionary "push" for us to step off the edge of the old and into a new paradigm may not be supported by the evolutionary winds of change.

I invite you to follow the evolutionary impulse and step off the edge and into a new Epoch for Humanity:

> *Come to the edge, He said. They said, We are afraid.*
> *Come to the edge, He said. They came. He pushed them*
> *. . . and they flew.*
>
> GUILLAUME APOLLINAIRE

REFERENCES

1. Oziris M. Stoltz, *Spiritual Awakening* (Bloomington, Ind.: Balboa Press, 2012).

THE POSTGROWTH ECONOMY

CHARLES EISENSTEIN

Charles Eisenstein is a teacher, speaker, and writer, focusing on themes of civilization, consciousness, money, and human cultural evolution. His writings for the web magazine *Reality Sandwich* have generated a vast online following. He speaks frequently at conferences and other events, and gives numerous interviews on radio and podcasts.

■ ■ ■

Immature ecosystems and immature human beings naturally pass through a stage of rapid growth before reaching a mature steady state. The same might be said for immature civilizations.

Our civilization is nearing the end of its childhood, during which we devoted our energies to growth. With each new scientific advance, the realm of human understanding expanded and the realm of the unknown, of the mysterious, shrank. With each new technology, the domestic realm, the sphere of human control, expanded and the realm of the wild shrank. And mirroring the entire ascent of humanity, the money realm, too, has grown; that is, the realm of property and the quantified transaction. The land became "real estate"; the stones underground became "resources"; even the genome, the electromagnetic spectrum, and the cultural heritage of stories, songs, and ideas became property of one sort or another.

We are now in a late stage of our final adolescent growth spurt. In science, the program of reductionistic certainty has hit insuperable limits;* our control-based technologies similarly generate diminishing returns

---

*The limits of reductionism first became apparent in the 1920s with quantum uncertainty and the subsequent proliferation of supposedly "fundamental" particles. The limitations of the axiomatic method itself became apparent in the 1930s with the work of Alan Turing, Kurt Gödel, and Alonzo Church. Later and most seriously, the discovery of the inherent unpredictability of most nonlinear systems imposed an insuperable barrier to the perfection of control-based technology. None of these discoveries has yet been fully digested, however.

(consider, for example, high-tech medicine or agricultural pesticides). But nowhere is it more obvious than in economics that we are reaching the limits of growth.

The ecological limits to growth are by now well-known: peak resources and the biosphere's limited capacity to absorb our waste. Equally significant are the social limits to growth. The atomization of society, the degradation of community, the replacement of nonmonetary social relationships of reciprocity, gift, and trust with the monetized relationships we call "services" bear a limit—the point at which there are no more services to be sold because everyone already pays for everything.

Politicians and economists alike hold economic growth as the primary goal of economic policy because the end of growth (or even its significant slowing) is disastrous in an interest-based monetary system. Debt rises faster than the ability to pay it back, wealth is concentrated in fewer and fewer hands, and capital races from one speculative bubble to another as the return on productive investment falls. The end of growth is at the root of the seemingly permanent financial crisis that started in 2008. It will not go away, though its manifestation will morph and metastasize in coming years.

With each new iteration of the crisis, we face a choice: either try harder to make the old system work or transition into a steady-state or degrowth economy. So far we've chosen the former every time: a somewhat schizophrenic combination of austerity so that the debts can be serviced a while longer, coupled with progrowth policies to squeeze a little more growth out of the environment. We can open new mines in the Amazon and Congo, we can excavate the Canadian tar sands, we can turn the subsistence peasants of the developing world into wage earners and consumers in the money economy. The alarm of policy makers at slowing growth is much like that of a parent who, seeing his adolescent teenager stop growing at age seventeen, feeds him artificial-growth hormones to prolong growth a little longer. The toll that takes on his body is no less than the toll on society and the environment that economic growth takes today.

Spurred by unstoppable crisis and grieved by the cost of growth for society and the planet, we will in the next eight years have a golden opportunity to make a different choice. We can choose to take on the role of a mature species.

The end of growth has a twofold meaning, depending on what one means by the *economy*. Tracing the word back to its root, *economy* simply means "ways of keeping house." If Earth is our home, the economy is that portion of nature that we turn toward human purposes. From this perspective, the end of growth would mean extracting less from nature and ultimately rejoining the circle of ecology, in which the waste of one species is food for another, and in which each species plays a role in the well-being of all.

In other words, the maturation of the human species means that the economy becomes an extension of, and not an exception to, ecology. The economic mechanisms to achieve this are within reach. It is not too much to hope that by 2020 we will see the following:

1. Green taxes or the equivalent that offset or internalize the cost of pollution and resource extraction. Pollution, CO_2 emissions, topsoil depletion, aquifer depletion, habitat destruction, and other environmental damage will become prohibitively expensive, creating an incentive to minimize these effects in production and distribution of goods. Powerful financial incentives will encourage zero-waste manufacturing, repair- and reuse-friendly design, green energy technologies, local production to avoid transport fuel costs, the restoration of ecosystems, and the remediation of toxic waste.

2. Payments to less-developed countries and regions for ecosystem services. In 2012, the remaining rain forests in the Amazon and the Congo are under threat by logging, mining, and ranching, as we continue to domesticate the wild. Our desire to reverse that trend needs a financial expression. In 2012, the developing countries complain that Western environmentalists are trying to hold them back from exploiting their resources to become rich like the West. Let us offer a different path to wealth. The rain forests, the waters, the reservoirs of biodiversity, the remaining indigenous tribes are all treasures of our planet. We are coming to value them

for their true worth. Let us hope that in 2020, our economic system reflects this.

In 2012, the big money is still in more efficient extraction, not in conservation or ecological healing. In the postgrowth era, that is going to change. No longer will our ideals conflict with our financial interests. We can see the beginnings of this shift already, as even those who wholeheartedly dedicate themselves to profit in the extractive model are having a difficult time succeeding. Even more important, fewer and fewer are doing it wholeheartedly. Two or three generations ago, bright young people could, with little self-deception, devote themselves fully to the grand project of humanity to conquer nature and bring civilization to every corner of the globe. Today that is impossible. We have had a change of heart, although we still live among institutions we've inherited from generations past. Hence the disconnect between our consciousness and our institutions, especially the institution of money.

What really must and will change, then, is the nature of money itself. Money is but a system of agreements about the meaning of symbols. It is, in other words, a story—the story of value. In 2012 money embodied the value of growth, for it was in the conversion of nature into commodities that wealth lay. The story in 2020 can be different. By shifting taxes onto pollution and resources, we can imbue money with the new, ecological values that we are adopting as we become mature members of the community of life.

The second meaning of the end of growth references conventional economics, which defines the economy as the totality of all monetized exchange. In this scheme, nonmonetary activity, such as sharing, gifts, voluntarism, subsistence farming, and civic participation, doesn't count. Economic growth has accompanied the erosion of such activities. Any time someone buys deli takeout rather than cooking for her family, any time someone sends his children to day care rather than caring for them at home himself, any time some people purchase music rather than making it together, the economy grows.

Reversing growth means reversing this trend—reclaiming parts of life from the world of money and doing things for ourselves and each other again. This is happening already, driven not by economic necessity but by the yearning to reclaim life from money. Consider, for example, the "reskilling" movement, in which people teach each other do-it-yourself skills that were once universal: food growing, preparation, and preservation; carpentry and home building; production of clothing; and herbal medicine and other home-based medicine. In intentional communities and even normal neighborhoods and towns, people are pooling resources so that each household no longer needs its own set of garden implements, power tools, and other infrequently used articles. Bike-share and car-share systems do the same. On the Internet, sites like Couchsurfing and Craigslist facilitate the flow of services unmediated by money, part of a sharing economy that removes the middleman and facilitates the free flow of music, video, images, and software. In the current system, all these trends are bad for the economy!

To many people, the *end of growth* evokes a kind of resignation, as if civilization itself will stagnate. "We will have to make do with less," is a common environmentalist mantra. But what, exactly, will we have less of? Only those things that involve the exchange of money. We will have less throwaway junk—but more durable, repairable, well-made goods. We will have fewer huge McMansions—but more high-density, walkable, and bikeable neighborhoods. We will have less food shipped cross-continent—but more fresh local food grown by people we know. In 2020 we will work less and play more, drive less and bike more, buy less and share more—and our lives will be the better for it.

Paradoxically, a degrowth economy is not an economy of greater scarcity—it is one of greater abundance. For something to have a non-zero price, it must, generally speaking, be scarce. For example, until clean drinking water was made artificially scarce through pollution and chlorination, it was generally free. Nowhere is impending abundance more apparent than in the digital realm. In 2012 the only way companies could exact a price for digital content was to create artificial scarcity through copyright protections, anticopying technology, and so forth. They seem to be fighting a losing battle, though, as sales have declined nearly every year since 1999. We can expect the same trend for other digital products like film, video, and software. Economic degrowth doesn't mean less stuff—it only means less stuff exchanged for money.

Abundance needn't be restricted to the virtual realm: most of the material scarcity people experience today reflects no fundamental scarcity but, rather, is an artifact of our system. For example, at present half the world wastes enough food to feed the other half, while high-tech chemical agriculture maximizes profits and yields per labor unit, but it is only one-half to one-third as productive as organic agriculture per hectare.* Another example: high-tech medical procedures are inherently scarce and expensive, but today we are seeing a reversal in the professionalization of medicine, as millions of semiprofessional and lay practitioners learn alternative and holistic modalities that are actually more effective than conventional treatments for many maladies of our time.

Of course, if more and more productive activity is happening outside the money system, there needs to be some way for society to support and reward people who are making nonmonetized contributions to society. The most direct way to do this is through a social wage, also known as a basic income, given equally to all citizens. It says "You don't have to work—but we trust that you want to." As such it encodes a different philosophy of human nature from that of traditional economics, recognizing the desire of each of us to contribute to something beyond ourselves (as all ecological beings do). This is yet another kind of abundance, another way in which the postgrowth transition is a transition from scarcity to abundance.

A social wage is also an expansion and universalization of the social welfare state—the very thing that governments around the world can apparently no longer afford. Why can't they afford it? Is it because worker productivity is lower than it once was? No. Technology and the productivity it facilitates have continued to progress. As always, fewer people can

---

*See, for example, studies catalogued by the Rodale Institute (Tim LaSalle, Paul Hepperly, and Amadou Diop, *The Organic Green Revolution* [Kutztown, Pa.: Rodale Institute, 2008]). Actually, I am being conservative here. Some permaculture researchers claim yields five or ten times higher than by conventional methods. See David Blume, "Food and Permaculture," www.whale.to/a/blume.html.

do more with less. Why, then, don't we enjoy increasing wealth and leisure? Why do we hear talk of cutting vacations, cutting pensions, raising the retirement age? There is no lack of resources, no lack of productivity; there is only a lack of money. Money is nothing but a set of agreements about the interpretation of bits in computers, and agreements can be changed.

More generally, why has the promise of an imminent age of leisure, current since the dawn of the Industrial Revolution, never come to pass? Again, the answer has to do with growth: at every turn, we have been compelled to find a way to consume more, rather than to work less. The money system dictates that choice, because a money system based on interest-bearing debt works only in a growth context.

When economic growth is insufficient to service growing debt burdens, the system can hobble on a little longer by hollowing out existing assets to service the debts. When the private assets of debtors are exhausted, their homes foreclosed, and their disposable income completely consumed by debt service, we shift the debts onto the public balance sheet so they can be serviced through public asset stripping: privatization, pension cuts, public salary reductions, and so forth. As these, too, approach exhaustion, the system becomes increasingly fragile. Like a frayed rope pulled tighter and tighter, it takes less and less force to snap it.

I have noticed that, in personal life, people seldom make substantial changes when their old way of doing things is still working. Societies operate the same way. In 2012 it was still possible to believe, if one were adept at self-deception, that normal is still normal, that the system is still working, that prosperity is around the corner, that the present crisis is a hiccup in the eternal trajectory of growth. With each new crisis, however, this belief gets harder to maintain. Indeed, many among the elite have ceased to believe it; they continue to play the game out of habit. "Extend and pretend," they whisper.

As the debt yoke weighs heavier and "normal" deteriorates, we will see in the next few years increasingly radical movements for economic democracy. Each iteration of the debt crisis will offer an opportunity for fundamental monetary reform. There are many ways, besides interest-bearing debt, to enact the social agreement we call money. Among the most promising is to subject money to a decay rate, known as demurrage, which erases the advantage that accrues to the owners of wealth. Developed by Silvio Gesell and Irving Fisher in the early twentieth century and revived in the 2000s by Bernard Lietaer, its modern implementation would be a liquidity charge, or negative interest rate, levied on bank reserves. Rather than hold onto reserves at a 5 percent interest rate, banks would willingly lend at low or zero interest, allowing credit to circulate in the absence of economic growth. Negative interest brings to money the ecological principle of decay. Ultimately, money that grows exponentially forever is inimical to an ecological, postgrowth economy. The details are beyond the scope of the present essay; suffice it to say that a demurrage-based system reverses the effects of interest: concentration of wealth, short-term thinking, and the growth imperative.*

At the present writing, even significant green taxes—let alone negative interest or a social wage—seem like too much to hope for. When things fall apart, however, what was once hopelessly radical becomes common sense. We are entering (in the West) a time of turbulence unprecedented in the last seventy years—and an opportunity for change that is unprecedented as well. We can see a glimpse of the future even now in the trends toward ecological manufacturing, green energy, permaculture farming, voluntary simplicity, reskilling, giving and sharing, localism, and the peer-to-peer revolution. Even under the hegemony of a money system that opposes them, these trends are ascending because they are aligned with our changing consciousness as an ecological species. By 2020, we will see that consciousness begin to infuse our basic economic institutions.

---

*For a detailed treatment of this topic, see chapter 12, "Negative-Interest Economics," in my book *Sacred Economics* (Eisenstein 2011).

A NEW SUPERPOWER

An Earth Voice Movement

DUANE ELGIN

Duane Elgin is an internationally recognized speaker, author, and social visionary who looks beneath the surface turbulence of our times to explore the deeper trends that are transforming our world. In 2006, Elgin received the Japanese Goi International Peace Award in recognition of his contribution to a global "vision, consciousness, and lifestyle" that fosters a "more sustainable and spiritual culture."

■ ■ ■

HUMANITY CONFRONTS A "SUPREME TEST"

The particular challenges facing humanity are well-recognized: climate disruption, income inequalities, species extinction, resource depletion, and so on. What is less well recognized is that these "adversity trends" are not isolated, but rather are part of a highly integrated system. For example, climate disruption and rising energy costs can disrupt global food supplies and produce widespread civic unrest. Individual trends can powerfully reinforce one another and produce consequences that were neither intended nor predicted. We are facing just such a time now—the perfect storm of a world in systems crisis with challenges so severe they will produce devastating breakdowns and offer the potential of catalyzing and profound breakthroughs.

This is our supreme test as a human community—our time of initiation, our rite of passage as a species. We will either learn how to pull together in common effort, or we will surely pull apart in devastating conflict. Which will it be? Can humanity wake up in time to the significance of this initiation and pull together in cooperation to create a future of sustainable prosperity?

A NEW SUPERPOWER IS EMERGING
ON THE EARTH

A new superpower is emerging on the Earth. This new superpower is the combined voice and conscience of the world's citizens mobilized through the global communications revolution. Although often chaotic, fragmented, and confusing, the emergence of social movements such as the Arab Spring and Occupy Wall Street demonstrates to ordinary citizens that their collective voice can have a powerful impact, particularly when expressed with the maturity and dignity of nonviolence.

When the people of the Earth are not simply on the receiving end of media as a collective witness to genocide, climate disruption, intense poverty, and the like, but also capable of offering a collective voice for change, then a new and powerful force for creative transformation will be unleashed in the world. As the people of the Earth learn how to use the new media tools to come together as a global community and express their collective voice, a new era in human development is being born.

A rapidly maturing voice for the Earth is emerging not a moment too soon, as, according to a broad consensus of researchers, the planet is measurably and rapidly approaching a profound tipping point leading to a ruinous future. It was humanity's ability to communicate that enabled us to coordinate our activities and consume resources at vast scales, producing an increasingly catastrophic level of human impact on the Earth. Now, our emerging capacity to communicate as movements in real time, with more life-affirming shared goals, has the potential to get us through the supreme test of these times. We are in a race with ourselves: Can we master the new communication channels fast enough to get ahead of the destruction that we are bringing to the Earth and humanity's future?

What kind of communication is required to give the citizens of the world an authentic collective voice? Critically important, it must be nearly instantaneous and global in scope. An authentic Earth Voice must reach the vast majority of the people of the Earth, and it must reach them virtually all at the same time! Seven billion or more people need to be able to offer their feedback about critical concerns if they are to feel part of an Earth Voice conversation.

When will it be feasible to have electronic gatherings that are global in scope and essentially instantaneous in receiving feedback, so that no one feels left out? This level of functioning of a "global nervous system" would have been completely unthinkable prior to the emergence of a new capacity for computing and networking that places information in the virtual cloud rather than on individual computers. As cloud computing accelerates, by the decade of the 2020s, the world will have the technologies with which to acquire real-time feedback and knowledge of humanity's sentiments and views. With these new capabilities and technologies, the identity and character of our species will be brought forth and made visible, enabling us to respond collectively to critical challenges.

As the world moves into the next phase of cloud computing, humanity will move into a new phase of transparency, self-reflection, and discovery. With communication capacities that are intensely interactive, highly intelligent, and virtually instantaneous, the citizens of the Earth will have a new superpower accessible to them—the power to communicate together and express common solidarity, for example, for a future of sustainable prosperity, freedom, and justice.

The new global superpower is developing fast and will continue to grow very rapidly. This Earth Voice movement—we might also call it the Gaian Voice or World Voice movement—is bringing all humans together in a shared process, all at the same time, enabling citizens to collectively give voice to concerns as well as compelling visions for a better world. When the global nervous system has developed to the point that we can all talk together at the same time as a human family (visualize instantaneous global voting by computer on major issues), we will visibly recognize that a new collective consciousness exists that can powerfully express citizens' shared desire to create a promising future for the Earth.

DO WE HAVE THE COLLECTIVE MATURITY TO STEP UP?

For the first time in human history, we are acquiring a way to listen to and talk with one another as members of one family. In awakening to ourselves as a planetary species and seeing ourselves directly and whole for the first time, we see that we have the potential for an evolutionary leap forward. However, although we have the technological capacity to communicate with ourselves as a species, this does not necessarily mean that we will rapidly discover our common humanity and destiny. The question remains as to whether we will have the collective maturity to seize this precious opportunity.

The Internet, combined with television, is creating a transparent world where injustices are impossible to hide. Just as a rising tide lifts all boats, so too does a rising level of global communication lift all injustices into the healing light of public awareness. What we see and hear through an Earth Voice process will surely challenge the emotional intelligence and maturity of the species. As humanity awakens to its collective history, deep psychic wounds will emerge that have festered through the ages. We will begin to hear the voices that have been ignored and the pain that has not been acknowledged. Our collective awakening will bring with it awareness of the dark shadows of human history in the form of racism, ethnic conflict, and religious discord. This process of coming face-to-face with our shadow will test the psyche and soul of our species as we search for reconciliation and renewal.

We are moving into a time of steel-gripped necessity, a time of intense planetary compression. In this generation, the world will become a superheated pressure cooker. The human family will be squeezed by unrelenting forces so unyielding, and the stresses they place on our world will be so extreme, that human civilization will either descend quickly into chaos or ascend in a spiraling process of profound transformation. On the one hand, if humanity is unwilling to work for the advancement of all, then the world will collapse into resource wars, and misery, poverty, and calamity will descend on the planet. On the other hand, unprecedented suffering may awaken humanity by burning through the unconscious denial, greed, and fear that now divide us. In encountering ourselves so directly and powerfully, a new and more mature human alloy may emerge from the furnace of these superheated decades. Our time of fiery transition may fuse the human family together with a new sense of identity and purpose that is strong enough to support the rebuilding of our lives to create a sustainable and meaningful future.

The suffering, distress, and anguish of these times can become a purifying fire that burns through ancient prejudices and hostilities to cleanse the soul of our species. We can expect no single, golden moment of reconciliation to descend on the planet; instead, waves of ecological calamity will reinforce periods of economic crisis, and both trends will be amplified by massive civil unrest. Instead of a single crescendo of crisis and conflict, there will likely be intense global conversation, momentary reconciliation, followed by disintegration, and then new conversations and reconciliations. In giving birth to a sustainable world civilization, humanity will likely move back and forth through cycles of contraction and relaxation. Only when we utterly exhaust ourselves will we burn through the barriers that separate us from our wholeness as a human family. Eventually, we will see that we have an unyielding choice between a badly injured (or even stillborn) planetary civilization and the birth of a bruised but relatively healthy human family and biosphere. In seeing and accepting responsibility for this inescapable choice, we will work to discover a common sense of reality, identity, and social purpose.

BUILDING THE FOUNDATION: LOCAL COMMUNITY VOICE MOVEMENTS

As metropolitan and regional networks of citizen communication are established, there will be a robust and resilient basis for supporting diverse Earth Voice initiatives. Within a decade, independent, transpartisan, and nonprofit Community Voice organizations will represent the rights and needs of major metropolitan areas and produce regular electronic town meetings with local to global impact.

This is not a fanciful or new idea. With the understanding that citizens legally own the airwaves at the community level, in 1987 in San Francisco, our nonprofit and transpartisan organization, Bay Voice, coproduced an electronic town meeting with the local ABC-TV station that was seen by over 300,000 people locally. Importantly, it also involved six votes from a preselected scientific sample of citizen viewers during the course of the hourlong, televised gathering. Within an hour, the sentiments of the Bay Area public were vividly clear.

With our transpartisan approach, a Community Voice organization has two key roles: first, to listen to the concerns of the community and second, to present those concerns for dialogue before the community in the form of electronic town meetings. The Community Voice organization itself is neutral and does no advocacy; rather, it serves as a vehicle for giving the community a voice in its own affairs and future.

If communities around the country were to form independent, transpartisan Community Voice organizations to launch local electronic town meetings, it would immediately revolutionize the conversation of democracy. The leadership of one community could inspire and catalyze other communities to create their own Community Voice organizations, and an entirely new layer of sustained and meaningful dialogue could sweep the country. Citizens could voice their views and help break through the gridlock now seen at the state, national, and international levels.

AN EARTH VOICE MOVEMENT

An Earth Voice movement based on transpartisan inclusiveness and the power of nonviolent global communication could emerge rapidly from the initiative of local Community Voice organizations. However, rather than emerging in a controlled or contained fashion, it seems more likely that an Earth Voice movement will coalesce out of the unique events and grassroots circumstances of life in different communities. Being uncontained and relatively spontaneous, it seems likely that many groups will seek in parallel to catalyze global conversations. This could develop into crowd-sourced global conversations with flash mobs of hundreds of millions—or even billions—of people joining in the dialogue. In this way, the collective intelligence of our global nervous system could take on a life of its own in a process that transcends artificial boundaries.

What will the human community want to talk about? Certainly there are global crises that require urgent and concerted action: climate disruption, energy transition, resource depletion, species extinction, and many more. Do the people of the Earth want more concerted and decisive action from their leaders? An Earth Voice movement with its synchronized and coherent communication could ensure that this message is delivered.

We are witnessing the awakening of the collective consciousness of the species as the Internet, television, cell phones, and other social media converge into an intelligent cloud of knowledge and communication. This intelligent cloud can support a truly global conversation for a promising future—an Earth Voice movement. The next great superpower will not be a nation or even a collection of nations; rather, it will be the billions of ordinary citizens who encircle the Earth and who are increasingly calling, with one voice, for unprecedented cooperation and creative action to bring practical vision and hope to our endangered planet.

WELL-BEING AND WELL-HAVING

MARCO ROVEDA

Marco Roveda is an entrepreneur, philosopher, and visionary. In 1978 he embraced biodynamic agriculture, and in 1981 established the Scaldasole Farm as the first organic food company in Italy. In 2000, he founded LifeGate, which became a meeting point for people and companies to focus on their ethical and sustainability objectives.

■ ■ ■

For some time now we have needed a big change, a step forward. For that to happen, we need, first and foremost, for our perception of well-being to change. All over the planet, people are obsessed with having things and are convinced that the accumulation of material goods will ensure their happiness. They don't realize how sterile and arid this concept is and, in fact, extend it to many areas of life, convinced that they are acting properly, fairly, and profitably.

But up to now, *well-being* has been wrongly confused with *well-having:* consumerism and materialism lead only to greed, a bulimic desire incapable of controlling itself without doing harm. The compulsive materialism to which we are slaves does not bring well-being.

However, we are seeing the birth of the need for a new awareness, a new spirituality associated with the growth of awareness, because we are beginning to understand that a new lifestyle is a positive and worthwhile thing. But how and when will we get there? The great change may occur in people first, and later in all our organizational and cultural systems, when we come to understand that real well-being comes from being well: most people will want to live with feeling, to give meaning to their own lives, to consume wisely, respecting the ecosystem and all forms of life. They will want to find a satisfying job, be honest with themselves and with others, and enjoy true friendships, while keeping at bay pain, fear, and rage, and living life joyfully.

At the end of the last century, it seemed that change might come faster. But then why are we so far behind? Because people are bipeds, cannibals, individualistic, slaves to the worst side of their brutality, they find it difficult to lift themselves up, to become spiritual. The past fifty years of compulsive consumerism have wiped out people's spirituality and made the path toward change even longer.

Change is necessary, but few people understand that: most of them are way down on the bottom, and very slow. It will happen, I am convinced of that, but it will take time: we'll make it, but we have to be aware that we are starting further back than it seemed.

SOCIAL MEDIA

The birth of consumerism and materialism is the result of an ambition for infinite, spasmodic growth, for the possession of things and material gain. It is no accident that we come from a panorama of information that was directed by just a few people, with just a few viewpoints, characterized solely by "well-having," that promote a single model of materialistic reference. To date, this conditioning has been the work of but a few people. Only a few people produced information and set trends and agendas. Only a few people put things into people's heads. Only a few opportunistic, heartless people managed information within a rigid framework that included only owning. In that system, beautiful people were those who knew how to demonstrate that they were capable of becoming rich and could lord it over others. What is the worst part of that? We were all partly complicit in it, and some of us still are.

Today a powerful current is developing, becoming ever bigger and breaking through the dikes of information managed by a few: that current is the Internet and the social networks. What the Internet and its associated media provide is not globalization, but freedom. People now have the ability to choose and are less conditioned than they once were. Now, thanks to the social networks, free society is facing off against a society of slaves: we are no longer slaves to a trend, a preestablished channel, or a preestablished agenda. Today we can all be agents and promoters of change.

The death of hegemony over information is an important step toward a new awareness: more and more people will free themselves from preestablished information and will feel with their own hands the sterility of "well-having." The Internet and the social networks today offer a wealth of possibilities for communication and content: while the old media were places and sets of practices aimed at communicating a single model, the new media are powerful tools aimed at conversation, at the exchange of ideas and new models of reference. What would happen if more and more people shared a new idea of happiness and well-being? Important steps would be taken toward a new awareness, toward change. Of course it will take time, but, step by step, we will be able to reemerge, to realize once again that we are not bipeds but people who can choose, think, share, and promote a new style of life.

WHAT PEOPLE WILL WANT

Sustainability will have to become the new lifestyle. The market produces what people want: people are the protagonists, and so it is necessary first of all for people to change, to acquire awareness. More and more people will want truth and reality, so companies will have to be more genuinely oriented toward People, Planet, Profit.

People, Planet, Profit—three links in the same chain. People's needs have to be met as part of the planet, thanks to profit, which is not an end in itself but aimed at responding to people's demands, so it must take into account the needs of the planet, without which there would be neither profit nor people.

People are the subject without which we would not be here having this discussion; people are not the means; they are the end. Satisfying people's needs, respect for individual human beings, and attention to the quality of life must be the crux of all reasoning and initiative. We are the people.

The planet is the theater of our existence; without the Earth, there is no life. It is the land on which we walk and live, the air we breathe, the food we eat: it is the water of life. If we do not consider the planet's needs, we undermine the very basis of our existence. We can no longer live off the ecosystem.

Profit is what makes it possible to satisfy the basic needs associated with survival; it is essential for living in contemporary society. But the time has come to understand that profit alone is not enough. Without the other two Ps, without taking into account both people and the planet, there is no harmony to life. There will not be any life, either.

Why, then, don't we combine the goal of making a profit—which is essential in the system we currently live in—with ethical values? Running a company in a way that yields a fair profit and at the same time produces something positive for the well-being of people and the planet is possible. *Ethical, ecosustainable,* and *equitable* must become inspiring principles for all companies involved in production systems, so they operate in a way that meets people's needs, with respect for environmental capital and the dignity of individuals.

A TURNAROUND IN SOCIAL ENTREPRENEURSHIP

A turnaround in business is not impossible. It requires close cooperation among market leaders. They have to join together not to banish competition but rather to implement socially and ecologically responsible practices in their own sector.

There are business leaders who may be ready to take this step. Many top companies are run by people or families who identify themselves with the company, whether they are founders or top managers. But today that is no longer enough. In the 1920s and '30s, no one would have suspected that pursuing business at all costs would have had such negative consequences. It was self-evident: society needed cars, gasoline, steel, and other goods, and big industry provided them. For business leaders, being "public-spirited" did not mean changing the orientation of their company but, rather, at most, ensuring fair treatment for workers and staff and supporting or taking on social causes.

Today it is no longer enough to "do good" with peripheral and marginal philanthropic gestures while remaining strictly dedicated to the objective of "doing well" in the market.

By 2020, it will be necessary for those who hold controlling power over large companies to become a driving force for the public good. Not with charity but by reorienting their companies.

The stakeholder in a company is society itself. By embracing that stakeholder, the private sector joins the ranks of social actors dedicated to the cause of humanity's well-being and ecological sustainability.

COMPANIES, FROM NOW TO 2020

People have begun to demand change from the corporate world. First, companies took up sustainability to promote their sales, then they realized that a People-Planet-Profit approach was essential for the company to be considered acceptable and to stay in the market.

The sustainable company will offer an opportunity for both people and companies: by publicizing and communicating virtuous behaviors, companies will promote the adoption of good practices by people and will introduce new standards in other companies.

A People-Planet-Profit approach will become inevitable. Some will get there with their hearts, and many will get there with their brains, but all will get there regardless.

SOCIAL ACUPUNCTURE

How Facilitating Integral Philanthropy Is the Future of Impactful Humanitarianism

JOSHUA RAYMOND FRENK
AND MARY ANN THOMPSON-FRENK

Joshua Raymond Frenk is the cofounder/vice president of the Memnosyne Institute (known as the Memnosyne Foundation from 2005 to 2012), where he oversees its international initiatives and local environmental initiatives. He currently serves as chairman of the Club of Budapest (COB) Americas, which is the only officially recognized COB chapter that is a collaborative initiative within an existing 501(c)3 (Memnosyne). He has directed several documentaries, including *Many Paths, One Source,* which won recognition at the Canadian International Film Festival of Non-Violence. Today he serves as a board member of the Mexic-Arte Museum, and is a member of the Sierra Club's John Muir Society.

Mary Ann Thompson-Frenk is the cofounder/president of the Memnosyne Institute (known as the Memnosyne Foundation from 2005 to 2012), and vice president of the Giordano Bruno University. She is a frequently requested international speaker and mediator and has received numerous awards for her humanitarian work, including Women that Soar's Philanthropy Award and the Aga Khan Foundation's Appreciation Award. Her writing has been published in various magazines, including *Philanthropy* and *Presidency Key Brief,* and she is currently finishing a book on photographer Gray Hawn, titled *Romancing Mexico.*

■ ■ ■

When our trailblazing friend, Dr. Ervin Laszlo, asked us to write a short essay on what philanthropy will need to evolve into by the year 2020 in order to be an effective positive force in the future, our first thoughts were of how globalization has changed the world and will continue to make humanity and the ecology of the planet all the more interconnected. We will need to develop the spiritual, sociological, and psychological software to balance the fast-evolving hardware of modern technology. For example, one cannot address issues relating to the environment without running head-on into economics, and one cannot make decisions in economics without exploring human rights, and human rights brings us to issues of interfaith relations, which then have a bearing on politics, and so forth.

If we attempt to make any type of sustainable change without first mapping the spiderweb of interconnections between the many issues at hand, we risk coming up with an incomplete solution. Add to this current scenario what Margot Brandenburg, the associate director of the Rockefeller Foundation, explained at UBS's inaugural 2012 Young Successors Program when she said, "The cost of repairing and addressing the world problems currently being faced far outsizes the combined budgets of philanthropy and the governments to address." Since it seems we have hit an era when the needs are increasing, but the amount of money encircling the globe is finite, we as a species are faced with a situation that provides an urgent call for global collaboration. Yet behind that urgency is an opportunity for an exciting new era of possibilities!

This scenario brings to mind a story told of a man who was given the chance to view both heaven and hell. In hell he saw a beautiful buffet, but all the people were starving because they were only permitted to eat with extremely long spoons and couldn't make the food reach their mouths. When he went to heaven, he was aghast to see the exact same scenario. But here, the people were all happy and sated because they were feeding each other. This is the exact situation we are now facing in the world. We have everything at our fingertips to be able to eradicate hunger, educate the poorest among us, and provide access to necessary resources and modern technologies. But to solve this, we are going to have to change our current way of thinking, which assigns resources to a set sphere, and begin exploring them in terms of being part of a whole planet. For example, according to the 2009 World Summit on Food Security, it would take $44 billion a year to end world hunger, yet $1,340 billion a year is currently spent on arms alone. If we look at the world's balance sheet, it becomes obvious that businesses hold the majority of the world's wealth today. However, with countries and industries now interdependent on each other's economic well-being, there is a growing recognition that cash must find a way to flow more freely or everyone loses.

This means that, in the future, humanitarian efforts will have to diversify their strategies and implementations, just as governments and corporations have. Redundancies will need to be removed, forcing duplicate organizations to merge, just as corporations have in the past. Collaborations between existing organizations that call on each other to do what they are the best at via combined strategies instead of attempting to keep needed programs under the umbrella of one nonprofit will be paramount. But the most crucial change required will be collaborations between for-profits and nonprofits. This is because of the current allocation of wealth.

But we don't have to create a new methodology from scratch; instead, we can borrow the collaborative business strategies of companies like Google and Sprint. Just as they didn't compromise their corporations' focus when they created a specialized cell phone, so can the nonprofits and for-profits of the near future forge mutually beneficial collaborations. Some for-profits, B-corporations, have been designed to do this from their inception by legally giving the welfare of humanity and the environment as much consideration as their shareholders' interests. Others, such as 7-Eleven, implemented strong profit-sharing programs in the 1950s and partnered with worthy causes, uniting their international clientele and employees around Muscular Dystrophy Association projects, starting in the 1960s. But today, a business needn't be huge to make a scalable, impactful difference. An example of B-corporations already doing this are the merged Giordano Bruno University/Wisdom University and GreenWorld Restoration LLC, which are together contributing world-class education in an off-grid school building that the nonprofit Memnosyne Institute is providing to the poorest areas of the world. To accomplish this task required negotiations that will count the first two years of donated services as marketing costs for the for-profits, during which the Memnosyne Institute will be endeavoring to raise funds to build future schools.

Most nonprofits, like Memnosyne, could never afford to put aside the millions of dollars necessary to develop the technologies, engineering, curriculum, and staff needed to design the universities or the ecodevelopment corporation. But by negotiating a collaborative win-win project with these two for-profits, the possibility of bringing world-class education to those most in need, and who are yet geographically inaccessible to conventional schools and universities, is now a true possibility. So now, imagine what other collaborations can be forged between nonprofits and for-profits that together will develop solutions spanning the globe!

The how-to behind getting your for-profit or nonprofit to explore the potential of applying integral theory to philanthropy is a simple one. One method that Memnosyne's Conscious Cultural Creators workshop uses is to illustrate how world challenges consist of interdependent connections, requiring holistic solutions in what we call a "yarn toss." You can use a web to map out and reveal common elements by literally tossing a ball of yarn between the many visionaries in the room. We used this modality for 350 people at the UN's Search for Common Ground's NEXUS Summit (July 20, 2011), and the results were the same as they were with the Cordoba Initiative's WISE (Women's Islamic Initiative in Spirituality and Equality) conference (May 25, 2009) of 300 Muslim women from 250 different countries, and the same as it was in a room full of today's leading scientists and thinkers at the Club of Budapest's Design Me a Planet Conference (July 11–16, 2011). It never fails to reveal to participants how their individual passions are interconnected with each other's concerns. This is an important step in forging collaborative strategies because it focuses funds directly into the areas with the most interconnections. We call it the Memnosyne Institute's social acupuncture process.

Recognizing the connections shared between humanity's many forms—institutions, religions, races, cultures, or anything else—is crucial; for, as the world continues to become more interdependent economically and politically, our environmental and sociological welfare will only be as healthy as our capacity to recognize and work within those webs. This means we have become each other's information resources and bear the responsibility for recognizing that, thanks to modern technology, we are the first generation of humanity that has no excuse for ignorance.

Make this reality less intimidating by asking, "What are the strategic points within a given society that, if focused on, will have the greatest impact?" This requires letting go of the lead-by-top-down approach, as leaders become facilitators of societal self-discovery. We cannot base our answers on individual knowledge bases that are trying to apply segmented answers to a holistic reality. This social acupuncture strategy is a sustainable way to impact challenges because it benefits from multiple perspectives, allowing us to see a problem three dimensionally, as opposed to wasting money on a symptom that will recur.

The key to ensuring a successful strategy is to design replicable systems from the beginning. Ask, "Can the strategy can be replicated by different people, cultures, and geographic regions?" Design systems that evolve. Ask, "Are the people the strategy serves empowered enough so they can evolve the system?" This is critical for a community's ownership and commitment, and for ensuring future innovations.

Measure a proposed strategy by Memnosyne's "Dartboard Measurement." Draw a three-ringed dartboard. Label it from the center out: Spiritual, Intellectual, Tangible. The ethics of a strategy come from the inside out, but the public's estimation of the project's value comes from the outside in. It is important to understand this difference during implementation. Implementation requires humility, an understanding that a collaborative process with those served yields enlightening answers for those seeking to help them. Celebrate their ingenuity! Let them know when their idea helped you to serve a community elsewhere because it will empower them to recognize that they are part of humanity's global family.

This is what distinguishes integral philanthropy. Traditional philanthropy seeks to alleviate a symptom. Integral philanthropy views an individual project as a systemic remedy: the people's transformation into conscious cultural creators (people who have become consciously aware of how their choices are creating their current culture economically, spiritually, environmentally, etc.), via the project, is the permanent empowerment that we seek.

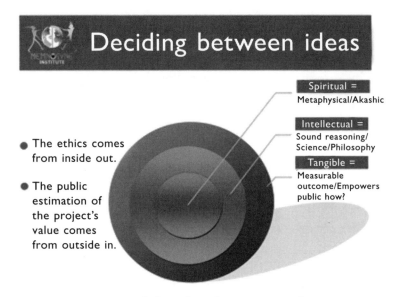

Memnosyne's "Dartboard Measurement"

To measure success, ask, "Do the people begin to recognize their own interdependence with each other?" "Do they initiate holistic strategies themselves?" and "Do they recognize their passions' interconnectedness with others?" To do these things is to put wisdom into action. While wisdom is often seen as an archaic concept, lacking in practicality, for conscious cultural creators, wisdom is an active, engaging practice that all people are capable of cultivating. It is the practical necessity of maintaining conscious awareness of how one's actions are creating today's and tomorrow's culture, based on our priorities. Social acupuncture is one of the most powerful tools for accomplishing this.

Therefore, understanding that the most sustainable difference an individual philanthropist, conscious capitalist, socially responsible investor, or nonprofit leader can make in the life of a community or individual is to empower them to become capable of social acupuncture themselves. We can now recognize that our job isn't just giving a man a fish, or even teaching a man to fish. Rather, in today's world, it is connecting that man to the fish market's leaders, those who weave the nets, those who provide the bait, finding alternatives for those who dispose of waste in the water, finding out what they need that the fisherman can provide more of when they do this, all the while educating ourselves by seeking to learn from the fisherman, inviting him to teach us about his water resources and the fish he relies on, making sure that our assumptions about his needs are correct, inviting him to the table to diagnose the problem, and sharing ownership of the solution with him. Do this, and the solution will be sustainable because he and his community feel ownership of it. Bring this understanding and process to the table with these scenarios and the humanitarian of 2020 will be revealed not as just the check writer, but as the facilitator who consciously creates webs within society so that humanity can evolve collaboratively. Do this, and see what an amazing world we can create together!

THE WAY TO THE SOLAR AGE

HAZEL HENDERSON

Hazel Henderson is the founder of Ethical Markets Media, LLC, and the creator and co−executive producer of its TV series. She is a futurist, an evolutionary economist, a worldwide syndicated columnist, and a consultant on sustainable development.

■ ■ ■

The multiple crises human societies experienced in the first decade of the twenty-first century must be acknowledged as results of our limited perceptions and occluded vision. Thus, these crises we experience are mirroring back to us the need to expand our awareness of the planet that hosts us, one among over 30 million other species that constitute its living biosphere. Stress is evolution's tool, feedback to expand our consciousness, which is now accelerating human learning processes far beyond traditional education and acculturation.

Thus we see the crises and breakdowns all around us as driving the necessary breakthroughs: in art, culture, science, technology, governance, politics, communications, production, services, awareness of ecological systems, and the place humans occupy in the web of life. We have seen in the various financial crises the inadequacy of conventional economics and the tools of finance it spawned based on the most unattractive human traits. These faulty economic models of human behavior almost mirror the seven deadly sins described in many spiritual traditions: envy, gluttony, greed (selfishness), lust (acquisitiveness), pride (competition), sloth, and wrath. No wonder our financial systems morphed into an unstable, error-prone global casino. Economics and its theories and models are rooted in the concept of scarcity, based on early human experiences of the natural world as dangerous and unforgiving and life as "nasty, brutish, and short," as political philosopher Thomas Hobbes characterized it in *The Leviathan.*

The promise of the twenty-first century is that many scales have now fallen from human eyes, along with the blinders of narrow perception and theorizing that psychologist Daniel Kahneman terms *theory-induced blindness*.[1] The uprisings of ordinary people in 2011 and 2012 threw off the shackles of many such earlier belief systems. The mysteries of money and economics are revealed as politics in disguise, as we see money being printed by the billions on our TV screens. Financiers do not provide capital, but are intermediaries between real producers who save money and the investors or borrowers who hope to use it well. Financiers claim that they could not have known the fatal weaknesses in their complex financial-engineering and illusory models. Yet those with more expansive awareness (including this author) had warned for decades about their inevitable failures. These were not "black swans" or "perfect storms." Self-induced blindness in economics textbooks still taught in business schools claim that social and environmental costs can be retracted from financial and company balance sheets and passed on to taxpayers, future generations, and the environment.

Today, humanity's collective awareness of the true conditions for our survival is continuing to expand exponentially, due to our globe-girdling communications tools and the new connectivity we have at our disposal. The window of opportunity is open wide. Our new scientific understanding grows: of our home planet Earth, and of ourselves, our behaviors, and the potential of our brains and our endocrine systems. We are not the lone individuals, as we assumed, but are all interconnected and interdependent—one human family sharing similar DNA, beyond any surface differences of skin tone, ethnicity, gender, or culture.[2]

As quantum physics and genetic research confirm the truth that we are all one, we embrace new visions and opportunities to grow in consciousness and compassion, as I describe in *Transitioning to the Future We Want* (forthcoming). We discover that we are wired by our hormones and mirror cells* for altruism and empathy. All this is now apparent, and a

---

*Colloquial term for *mirror neuron,* a neuron that fires both when an animal acts and when the animal observes the same action performed by another. Thus, the neuron "mirrors" the behavior of the other, as though the observer were acting.

more peaceful, harmonious future is seen as viable and indeed the basis of our survival. The work of biologist Charles Darwin has been reevaluated by scientists (theDarwinProject.com). Among other findings, this research shows that Darwin did not invent the poisonous phrase *the survival of the fittest,* on which the false concepts of Social Darwinism were constructed.[3] In *Darwin's Lost Theory of Love* (iUnivers, 2000), psychologist David Loye explores Darwin's theories that human survival skills lay primarily in our ability to bond with each other, care, and share, which he believed would lead to the evolution of altruism.

Money was a wonderful human innovation, but it is not wealth; rather, it's a metric to track and keep score of human transactions. Compound interest is a mathematical illusion that counters the Second Law of Thermodynamics, as I discussed in *Politics of the Solar Age* (New York: Doubleday, 1981). Traditional societies have known this for centuries. As unrepayable debts built up in societies throughout history, religious leaders and kings canceled them in Jubilees. The Jubilee 2000 movement prompted the World Bank to cancel the debts of the highly indebted Heavily Indebted Poor Countries (HIPC) in Africa. Money creation and credit allocation simply based on the trust of banks and governments was exposed as corrupt and is leading to the reforms and widespread currency innovations at all levels still evolving today.

Humanity is becoming conscious that "We are all one," as taught in most religious traditions and books, including *The Ways and Power of Love* by Pitirim Sorokin (West Conshohocken, Pa.: Templeton Foundation Press, 1954, 2002). This orchestration of innovation and higher consciousness, together with countless movements of compassionate action, can help humanity to endure the rigors and painful adjustments of the transition to fairer, more ethical, global, green economies, envisioned for decades and now becoming a reality.

These possibilities were explored by Sorokin, who formed his Center for Creative Altruism at Harvard University. I have explored elsewhere the extent of the "Love Economy," that fundamental base of human survival in the unpaid "women's" work of caring, sharing, volunteering, and community service. All this is now joined by the open-source and peer-to-peer movements growing out of digital technology's opportunities and described by Don Tapscott in *Wikinomics* (New York, Atlantic Books, 2007). Just as these unpaid sectors are excluded from GDP, so is the productive work of nature, which supports all life. Today, these unpaid sectors of direct information-based trading, together with the Love Economies, are larger than the official money-using, GDP-measured sectors of the world.[4]

As we expand our awareness of our true productive capabilities and the daily influx of free photons from our Mother Star, the sun, we see that we live not in conditions of scarcity but of abundance! In our Information Age, we experience this abundance in sharing: for example, if I give you information, you have gained and I have lost nothing. We are both richer!

The Earth provides us and all species with our life-giving resources. The sun showers us with trillions of photons freely every day. Enough sunlight falls on the Earth in just one hour to meet world energy demands for a whole year.[5] Green plants innovated methods of capturing these photons and turning them into food. Their technology is photosynthesis, using the chloroplasts in their cells to turn sunlight into forms of sugar and other carbohydrates, which form the basis of our human food supply. Bees and other insects helped by fertilizing our crops, fruits, nuts, and seeds.

As coal, oil, gas, and uranium began to pollute our planet and atmosphere, we humans began looking up—and appreciating our life-giving sun, which actually powers our planet and sustains all life in our biosphere. Humans began to look at plants, learning from their successes at capturing the sun's rays, asking nature how millions of life-forms have learned how to survive over 3 billion years, coexisting and thriving on the sun's abundant free energy. Today, a revolution in science is learning to respect nature as the great innovator. We are harvesting the sun's rays in many ways—from wind, from water, from direct capture of solar rays on rooftops, and in central power towers, creating steam to drive turbines and create electricity for our transport and factories. We are learning how nature maximizes efficiency, recycling and reusing all energy and materials, and leaving no waste or pollution.

As we humans learn to mimic nature's billion years of experimentation and innovation, we are progressing. Our future prospects are looking up. Since 2007, our Green Transition Scoreboard has tracked individual and private investments in creating greener, cleaner economies globally at $3.3 trillion! If we continue to invest at least $1 trillion per year until 2020, we will be leaving the fossil-fueled Industrial Era and entering the Solar Age! Our Green Transition Scoreboard maps the shift from the fossil-fueled Industrial Era to the Solar Age. As investors realize the nature of real wealth, they are moving their money to invest in the cleaner, greener, information-rich green sectors worldwide.

This story of mass learning, planetary awareness, and systems thinking was evident at Rio+20 and moved its 193 UN-member countries toward greener, cleaner, information-rich economies. This UN summit marked the twentieth anniversary of the Earth Summit in 1992 and the fortieth anniversary of the first one in Stockholm in 1972. I participated in all three of these summits and witnessed thousands of NGOs teaching bureaucrats about global and local issues, yet to reach media or governments' attention. Rio+20 followed those on climate, health, cities, population, oceans, and social inclusion. They have led to treaties on protecting human rights, children, women, migrating birds, endangered species, and forests; promoting access to communications, education, and health for all; reducing poverty; and, in 2000, the UN's Millennium Development Goals.

Cynics delight in ridiculing the UN, yet the past fifty years of official global conferences, and hundreds of thousands more meetings by NGOs, concerned business and investor groups, environmentalists, and social justice networks of the World Social Forum, nevertheless helped produce the new systems thinking and curriculum now entering academia, governments, and the new media. The human family is awakening to how we and 30 million species sharing planet Earth have innovated, thrived, and survived for 3.8 billion years. Education has burst out from academia into real-time learning online.* Janine Benyus, with her 1997 book *Biomimicry* (New York: William Morrow) and her Biomimicry 3.8 group of scientists around the world, teach how our living biosphere maintains itself and evolves with biomimicry workshops. The insanity of burdening

---

*See Alexander Laszlo and Jean Russell's "Thrivable Education" essay in this section.

children with unrepayable debt to acquire often obsolete information has been exposed in the United States, where student debt has reached an unrepayable $1 trillion in an economy with widespread unemployment.

Rio+20 provided many other learning experiences, together with over 55,000 NGOs. We are witnessing everywhere the acceleration of global learning—speeded up by all the new communications tools we have invented. Since I wrote *Creating Alternative Futures* (New York: Berkley Pub. Corp, 1978), I have tracked this human story and our race between expanding our awareness and the destructive forces threatening our common future. *The Politics of the Solar Age* I foresaw in 1981 is now upon us! The good news is that we are connecting the dots. Janine Benyus and I, and our companies, have joined forces and created our Principles for Ethical Biomimicry Finance for future responsible investing.

In a very real way, the space programs since the 1960s had set the stage for humanity's growing awareness of our blue planet, seen for the first time floating in the blackness of space. U.S. astronaut Sally Ride launched Mission to Planet Earth in the 1980s, which birthed the new interdisciplinary Earth systems science and its satellite views of polluted estuaries and growing deserts. This led to GPS, Google Earth, and the first UN agreements on climate change in Rio in 1992 and Kyoto in 1998. The Millennium Development Goals and the UN Global Compact followed in 2000, spurred by the World Wildlife Federation's Living Planet Index, the UN Millennium Ecosystem Assessments and the Ecological Footprint, now used widely and in product labeling. In 2009, the UN launched the Green Economy Initiative and the Global Green New Deal. The Economics of Ecosystems and Biodiversity measures nature's productivity.[6]

People started reinvesting in their own communities, created local currencies, flocked to local credit unions, farmers' markets, and time banks.* The still-visible love and gift economies undergird the thriving local living economies we can rely on as safety nets in likely future global meltdowns. These, together with the relocalizing of banks and investing,

---

*Time banking is a pattern of reciprocal service exchange that uses units of time as currency. It is an example of an alternative monetary system. A time bank, also known as a service exchange, is a community that practices time banking.

can again become the mainstay of national economies. E. F. Schumacher, whose *Small Is Beautiful* was published in 1973 (New York: Harper & Row), and who wrote the foreword to my first book, would be proud of his legacy. Microcredit had blossomed worldwide since the 1970s with pioneering efforts by the Grameen Bank and the BRAC* in Bangladesh; the Women's World Banking network in many African, Asian, and other countries; and ACCION and others in Latin America. In our new century, women also are recognized as peacemakers and included in peace negotiations as the main actors in conflict resolution worldwide.

My vision is that women and men in partnership can become fully conscious and can continue to coevolve with other life on this planet as we have done successfully for the past 3.8 billion years. The key, as my Buddhist friends say, is "waking up" to our fullest consciousness.

REFERENCES

1. Daniel Kahneman, *Thinking Fast and Slow* (New York: Farrar, Straus and Giroux, 2011).
2. See, for example, Bryan Sykes, *DNA USA* (New York: Liveright, 2012).
3. Hazel Henderson, *Ethical Markets: Growing the Green Economy* (White River Junction, Vt.: Chelsea Green, 2007), 230.
4. Hazel Henderson, *Transitioning to the Future We Want* (London: ICAEW and Tomorrow's Company, 2013).
5. "Green Transition Scoreboard," EthicalMarketsMedia, www.youtube.com/user/EthicalMarketsMedia/featured (accessed January 15, 2013).
6. "The Economics of Ecosystems and Biodiversity: Mainstreaming the Economics of Nature: A Synthesis of the Approach, Conclusions and Recommendations of TEEB" (Geneva, Switzerland: TEEB, 2010).

---

*BRAC is a development organization, founded in Bangladesh in 1972, dedicated to alleviating poverty by empowering the poor to bring about change in their own lives.

THRIVABLE EDUCATION

ALEXANDER LASZLO AND JEAN RUSSELL

Alexander Laszlo, Ph.D., is cofounder and president of Syntony Quest, and professor of systems science and evolutionary development at a number of graduate schools. He is president of the International Society for the Systems Sciences (ISSS), and executive fellow at the Center for Advanced Study of the Giordano Bruno University. He serves on the editorial boards of four international research journals, is an active member of several systems sciences societies, and has authored a total of more than sixty journal articles, books, and encyclopedia entries.

Jean Russell is founder of Thrivable Inc., an accelerator for the new economy, and cofounder of ci2iglobal, which lubricates knowledge sharing across the social change movement. She serves as a catalyst and social-ecosystem designer. Founder of the thrivability movement and a premier expert on collective thriving, she speaks to and with change agents, innovators, builders, and edge riders. She edited and published, *Thrivability: A Collaborative Sketch* with sixty-five contributors.

■ ■ ■

The current need to educate a planetary citizenry under conditions relevant to the living context of our planet drives us toward thrivable education. It takes its cue from the life sciences—biomimicry, ecosystem studies, permaculture, and the like—and from the sciences of complexity—complex adaptive systems theory, second-order cybernetics, social systems dynamics, and similar fields.

The crumbling educational system of the past disconnects the learner from life through mechanistic worldviews. Factory-style education—where students are grouped according to age, learn at the same pace as determined by the conveyor belt of course delivery, and have knowledge instilled in them through rote memorization and regular testing—has entirely ceased to serve the needs of our rapidly evolving age. As Hazel Henderson points out in the preceding essay, student debt in the United States exceeds $1 trillion, burdening learners with excessive loans for an education that no longer serves their needs. Graduation from this system fails to ensure the lifelong-learning competencies necessary for constructive engagement with an ever-changing world. Given the technological limitations and cultural constraints of the past, the scaling of education through the mechanization of this process did indeed serve the needs of the time as well as it could. But times have changed, and so have educational technologies and paradigms.

All over the world, more dynamic, systemic, evolutionary systems of learning have begun to flourish. In the preceding essay, Henderson describes how "the new systems thinking and curriculum now entering academia, governments, and the new media . . . [have] burst out from academia into real-time learning online." Both young people and adults crave learning that is fun, engaging, challenging, and connects them to the pulse of life. As we learn more about how the human brain functions, we begin to feed our need for dwelling in stories (how the mind remembers) and playing to human incentives by engaging in game dynamics. What comes about through the process known as the gamification of education is best termed ludic learning.

Gaming culture inspires learning globally. Massively Multiplayer Online Games (MMOGs) bring people together to collaborate for shared wins. The pleasurable rewards from this activity affect the expectations of young people. Where once we were "cheating" by sharing our knowledge with others, we now recognize such behavior as the sort of desirable collaboration and networked intelligence crucial for real-world action. Such interactive frames bring with them a new literacy. Icons representing various system states and dynamic readouts of environmental conditions provide visual analogues of key indicators of the flux and flow of health in the virtual environment, creating a tapestry of symbolic meaning akin to how fighter pilots learn to process information from their jet consoles. It should be no surprise then that students who thrive in these dynamic and complex environments, rewiring their brains for such mental gymnastics, suffer and languish when asked to process the stultifyingly static information that comes off printed text and linear language.

As a species, we now strive toward human and ecosystem flourishing—not as an educational vocation or pastime, but as an increasingly recognized prerequisite for all of humanity to continue to coexist in and contribute to the web of life on Earth. We crave thrivability: the ability to thrive, for ourselves and our children. The need to be adaptive and agile in changing environments is becoming ever more clear.

Thrivability gives well-being and conviviality primacy. To thrive is to create more value than you consume; to be generative by expanding, enriching, or evolving the systems within which you live. Rather than static, highly specialized knowledge, which we have learned how to develop quite proficiently, we lean toward variety and integration in service of conviviality with all the living beings and life-support systems in our milieu.

Thrivability builds on the lessons and wisdom of sustainability. It transcends sustainability partly because it adds a framework for understanding how to navigate complexity in turbulent environments. Drawing on lessons from the life sciences and from quantum-field theory and scalar-field theory, thrivable education teaches about emergence in complex adaptive systems. It does so by preparing learners for multiple roles in their living ecosystems—roles that naturally involve a panarchy of relationships. Panarchy, as an organizing principle of complex adaptive systems, suggests that all systems embed and are embedded in dynamic contexts involving other systems, and that, when effectively—and affectively—aligned, they self-organize for optimal functionality. This intertwingling* of systemic relations leads to a manifest conviviality in thriving systems and the ecosystems that embed them.

One of the interesting insights into thrivability from contemporary science has to do with the phenomenon of coherence in thriving systems. It is now understood that liquid water is made up of networks of "coherence domains"—regions in which the molecules act in phase. This is called coherence. What is interesting and particularly significant for the

---

Intertwingling is a term coined by Theodor Holm Nelson in 1974 that conjoins "mingled" and "intertwined" to indicate a state of deep and complex connectedness and interpenetration.

dynamics of thrivability that give rise to conviviality is that when sets of coherence domains come into coherence among themselves, an emergent phenomenon known as "super-coherence" occurs. As it turns out, only dissipative systems—ones capable of exporting to their environment the entropy they produce—are capable of super-coherence. A system composed of super-coherent subsystems is highly resonant. That is, it carries, sustains, and conveys patterns of health and well-being as long as it is not actively destabilized in its resonant milieu. When brought to the level of human social and societal systems, this phenomenon is expressed in terms of hyperconnectivity.

Ross Dawson describes the phenomenon of hyperconnectivity as an emergent property of our globalizing sets of relationships.[1] As we become ever more intertwingled, the potential for super-coherence among the social systems in which we live, conduct business, and manipulate our environment offers the promise of deep conviviality with such high levels of thrivability as could only be ascribed to the emergence of societal superorganisms. These living networks of convivial communities of practice, of interest, and of place lay the foundation for a global eco-civilization in which humanity takes on the role of curators of planetary thrivability.

But it could just as easily go in the other direction. What emerges as synergetic intertwinglement when thrivability is consciously curated can degrade toward negative synergetic entanglement when myopic and egocentric perspectives dominate. Without an educational framework that nurtures super-coherence in our societal systems, and coherence at the individual level of our psychoemotional selves, we run the risk of creating ever-larger networks of dysfunctionality.

Key to thrivable education is the focus on the coherence domains of the learners in the context of their living environment. There are four coherence domains for human thrivability:

- At the first coherence domain—conviviality with oneself; personal or internal thrivability—the practices involve centering, quieting the monkey mind, listening with every cell of our being. These practices cultivate intuition, empathy, compassion, insight that matches outsight, and a willingness to explore and follow our deepest calling.

- At the second coherence domain—conviviality with others; community or interpersonal thrivability—the practice involves deep dialogue and collaboration. We come together to learn with and from each other and to engage in coordinated action with considerateness, openness, and joy to enable collective wisdom.

- At the third coherence domain—conviviality with nature; ecosystemic or transpersonal sustainability—the practices involve communing; listening to the messages of all beings (whether they be waterfalls, animals, or galaxies) and acknowledging our interdependence and ultimate unity.

- At the fourth coherence domain—conviviality with the flows of being and becoming; evolutionary or integral thrivability—the practices involve learning to read the patterns of change of which we are a part; becoming familiar with the improvisational jam session that nature has been playing since time immemorial. These practices cultivate our ability to sing and dance our own path into existence in harmony with the grand patterns of cosmic creation and to participate in the ongoing flourishing of life.

Super-coherence occurs when all four coherence domains become coherently aligned in daily practice, resulting in an integral engagement with thrivability. As such, thrivability education is keyed to these practices—always promoting a spirit of innovation in the learner. Just as the survival imperative for every business is to have a clear answer to the question, "Innovate for what?," so the thrival imperative for every educational institution is to have a clear answer to the question, "Educate for what?"*

The Massive Open Online Course (MOOC) of the early second decade of the twenty-first century will give way to more direction-generating educational models in subsequent decades.[2] There have been many efforts to massify and democratize education in the early 2010s,

---

*For more on the thrival imperative, see Paul Radde's book *Thrival!* (Austin, Texas: Path Lighter Press, 2002).

ranging from online academies to prestigious multiuniversity collaborations that offer free and remarkable online libraries of lessons worth sharing. Additionally, cross-organizational standards will be devised to help learners and those who work with them to understand proficiencies across various programs, online or offline.

Yet few provide education explicitly dedicated to thrivability. One example of this educational orientation that emerged at the beginning of the 2010s is the revolutionary educational offering of the Giordano Bruno University (aka, the Giordano Bruno GlobalShift University; the Giordano Bruno World University). The stated educational purpose of the university is "to create informed and ethical agents of change who will bring a new consciousness, a fresh voice, and up-to-date thinking to the international community, transforming obsolete paradigms and empowering the co-creation of an equitable, responsible, and sustainable world." Such an education creates futures—specifically, thrivable futures. More and more, this will become the pathway for a postrelativistic, visionary, and future-creating educational paradigm that reverses the trend toward "feel good" education based on teaching whatever the market demands.

As we shift from single-solution, positivistic forms of learning to evolutionary biomemetic frames where learners coevolve solutions in all four coherence domains, students learn with fewer preset answers and more open inquiries. Both young students and adult learners learn in peer groups: peer-to-peer discovery facilitated by learning guides and active listeners, rather than by traditional subject matter experts. Organizations such as the Peer to Peer Foundation* are leading the way with processes that facilitate the self-knowledge and self-awareness of this movement toward peer learning and practice. Self-organizing initiatives can evolve rapidly and powerfully with such new orientations, with organizations like Escuela Nueva (New School)† enabling child-centered collaborative learning for more than 5 million educationally disenfranchised people living in rural and urban poverty.

Decades from now, we will consider thrivable education as that

*See http://p2pfoundation.net
†See www.escuelanueva.org/portal

which enables us to curate and nurture the past, present, and future of ecosystem relationships and health. As we develop greater relational intelligence of flows, using pattern recognition and evolutionary systems frameworks, we move away from static and egocentric knowledge production. We become a manifest form of networked intelligence, avoiding the myopia that resulted from factory-based education and specialization.

Thrivable education, while encouraging access to facts and data, focuses on how information is integrated and discerned. Rather than producing many graduates with the same knowledge, thrivable education nurtures diverse forms of intelligence and the ability to connect these forms in myriad ways to adapt to current and emerging conditions as needed. The shift comes not from imposed changes from the management sector of education, but rather as demanded and prototyped at the edges of contemporary learning environments. This is exactly what is happening, as we witness exciting innovations emerging the world over.

Will Varey, from Australia, is a professional practitioner of sustainability and social strategic planning, specializing in the psychodynamics of generative organizational change. He is creating an area of learning based on "the systemic study of the nature of wellness and its causes, processes, development and consequences in emergent systems," in contrast to the prevalent study of sick and dying systems and how to prevent them.[3] This shift from a focus on pathology is termed *apithology*, combining the Latin prefix *apic-* (indicating "apex") with the suffix *-logy* (meaning "the study of"). When applied to the area of educational concerns, apithology becomes apithagogy: "an inquiry into learning to discover the learning needs of a changing humanity as it learns about itself."*

Another example of emerging innovation in thrivable education comes from the work of systemic thinker and social entrepreneur Violeta Bulc of Slovenia and the InCo Movement she has started. As she says, the InCo Movement arose as "a movement for an innovative breakthrough whose aim is to promote active interstructural dialogue

---

*This is Varey's definition, which appears on http://apithagogy.blogspot.com.

and development of tools for sustainable development of an innovative society."[4] Yet another example comes from management consultant and educator Stefan Blachfellner's work out of Austria on the Change the Game Initiative (GTC). CTG was conceived as an umbrella movement for initiatives of all types that seek to "discover the interdependence between ethics and innovation and its impact on the social, ecological, and economic sustainability of business models, organizations, and societies at large."[5] Yet another innovator in the field, the Mycelium School of Asheville, North Carolina, fosters the skills for learners to address root causes of social and environmental concerns while encouraging a rich, textured awareness of self.*

In 2013, an initiative of the International Society for the Systems Sciences (ISSS) focuses on scaffolding a Global Evolutionary Learning Laboratory (GELL) for planetary thrivability. As a fundamentally educational initiative, the fifty-seventh annual conference of the ISSS focuses on Curating the Conditions for a Thrivable Planet: Systemic Leverage Points for Emerging a Global Eco-Civilization. It aims to "contribute to an evolutionary narrative of the next phase of human civilization in a time of global personal awakening."[6]

Efforts such as these are becoming increasingly prevalent and serve to underscore the need for thrivable education. The International Conferences on Collaboration and Intelligence in Blended Learning (CIBL) provide yet another example of emerging orientations to thrivable systems based on convivial relationships in learning processes.†

In a world where any documented fact can reach anyone with access to the Internet, the memorization of facts ceases to be a differentiator between individuals. Instead, the limited resource has become the creative combination, integration, and useful application of knowledge into networked production and customization. Thrivable education addresses the need for attention to this resource, and cultivates it through learning platforms that situate lifelong learners in a world that is relevant and meaningful to them—now and in the future.

---

*See www.myceliumschool.org.
†See http://ktw.mimos.my/cibl2012.

REFERENCES

1. Ross Dawson, "Autopoiesis and How Hyper-connectivity Is Literally Bringing the Networks to Life," Trends in the Living Networks, May 11, 2010, http://rossdawsonblog.com/weblog/archives/2010/05/autopoiesis_and.html (accessed June 26, 2012).
2. See A. McAuley, B. Stewart, G. Siemens, and D. Cormier, "The MOOC Model for Digital Practice," University of Prince Edward Island, Social Sciences and Humanities Research Council's Knowledge Synthesis Grants on the Digital Economy, 2010.
3. "Apithology" at www.emrgnc.com.au/apithology.htm (accessed January 15, 2013).
4. "InCo Movement for an Innovative Breakthrough," InCo Movement, www.incomovement.eu (accessed January 15, 2013).
5. "An Open Innovation Hub for Ethics & Strategic Leadership," Change the Game Initiative, www.changethegame.org (accessed January 15, 2013).
6. "Origin and Purpose of the ISSS," International Society for the Systems Sciences, www.isss.org/world (accessed January 15, 2013).

FROM THE VANTAGE POINT

SCOTT NOPPE-BRANDON

Scott Noppe-Brandon is an internationally known speaker and author on the critical role of imaginative thinking, creative action, and innovative outcomes (ICI) across commerce, culture, and education. For over twenty years Scott served as executive director of the Lincoln Center Institute. His current professional endeavor is the creation of the combined non-profit educational institute called EmaginationEd, Inc., and the for-profit business-based consulting and design firm called Squiggle Consulting LLC. He sits on several education and media boards; is a senior advisor for the Council on Competitiveness; and is co-author of Imagination First (selected top 1 percent of business books by EBSCO and SUCCESS Books) as well as the lead author of numerous chapters, essays, Update articles, and blogs. At LCI, Scott started the highly regarded Imagination Conversations and is co-creating the new media series Designing Imagination.

■ ■ ■

In retrospect, if there is one thing that we as individuals and as communities did not adequately address in 2012, it's that all the features of our society, all our challenges, and all the solutions to the problems were inextricably connected. Nothing exists or has ever existed in a vacuum. All systems, whether environmental, technological, communication, or energy-based: they all coexist and drive each other—toward catastrophic ends or toward the proverbial light at the end of the tunnel. Which way they go depends on who's at the wheel, and by 2012 it was very clear that all of us—everyone on the planet—were at the wheel. This is not an argument for a populist perspective but rather what I pray is a pragmatic view toward change. Sustainable product development and human development, the noun and the verb of the lived experience, need to be in equal focus. The United Nations Report on Human Development 2011 highlights this point by emphasizing that sustainability is "fundamentally about how we choose to live our lives."

For hundreds of years, at least in the Western-influenced world, we were taught to focus on our specialties and contribute what we could, without meddling in others' affairs. As the responsibilities escalated, we began to panic: We were willing to support good ideas, but to have to be part of all of them? Wasn't our daily grind complicated enough? Do I really have to monitor what my senator does to represent my interests? Do I have to separate my recyclables, protect my children from secondhand smoke, make sure that my pension plan is judiciously invested and that no one has hacked into my computer?

Yes, I do.

Bear with me. This vantage point has a reason. My own focus, throughout my career, has been in the field of education. My interest is not just what we teach but why we teach and how we teach. In short, what it means to educate and to be educated. I began my career by bringing the arts to the classrooms, because they were something I loved, so it seemed to me that life was less meaningful without them. Subconsciously, a larger concept was brewing inside me ever since I first studied the arts in the 1970s. In the 1990s, when we were already beset by crises—economic, political, societal—and everyone understood that a reformed education was imperative if solutions were to be found, I articulated that concept. It was that the arts did not exist in a vacuum: they were a fantastic medium that opened unsuspected doors to learning. Jiddu Krishnamurti, who rejected the role of teacher, educated awfully well. He said, "To see is to act." Guided by the poetic advice from Paul Cézanne, that "our eyes see the front of the painting, but imagination curves to the other side," I acted.

This belief evolved into the theory that if we are to value and promote innovation, we would do well by starting with imagination. In fact, imagination, creativity, and innovation are all parts of a whole. In the course of making the imagination into something that we could bring to educators as a tangible subject to teach, my colleagues and I learned a lot about it. We learned that it had been a bone of contention among thinkers from ancient civilizations to René Descartes, who thought it an enemy of reason. In general, the imagination had a rather dismal reputation. It was vague, it was dangerous, it was irrational; also, it was fickle, because very few had it anyway, and those who did tended to be shady characters.

But attitudes had begun to change by the early 2000s, with great help from unexpected sources: science, national security, and commerce. Research papers began to abound, addressing the premise that much of what we all do as part of our daily routine are acts of imagination. The Museum of Natural History in New York featured a disarmingly accessible exhibit on the subject. National security agencies blamed the "lack of imagination" for terrorist attacks that could have been predicted and prevented. Business leaders spoke convincingly about the need for a creative workforce.

With my leadership, my colleagues and I organized national forums in which people of all sectors—not just educators, but businesspeople, spiritual leaders, neuroscientists, legists, military leaders, artists, and others—discussed imagination, creativity, and innovation: what it was in their eyes, how it had served them, and how it could serve the whole community. I coauthored a book about it,* which strove to harvest new perspectives and dispel many myths, chief among them that imagination was not something sufficiently concrete to be taught, and that you either had it or you didn't. Nonsense, said our book, and "Nonsense," said the science.

This concept gained supporters at a fantastic rate. But, simultaneously, a strange thing happened: most, even among those who had joined in the promotion of imagination, often did not connect it to other processes of the human brain and lived experience, even though the processes were inherently imaginative. The workforce, the diplomacy, and the sciences all spoke increasingly about the need for innovative and creative minds. Consider these bullets from the European Commission on a strategic framework for EU Member States cooperation in education and training, known as "ET 2020":

Imagination First: Unlocking the Power of Possibility by Eric Liu and Scott Noppe-Brandon (2011).

- Making lifelong learning and mobility a reality
- Improving the quality and efficiency of education and training
- Promoting equity, social cohesion, and active citizenship
- Enhancing creativity and innovation, including entrepreneurship, at all levels of education and training

I agree wholeheartedly with all of the above. Note the mention of creativity and innovation—but where is imagination? If we are to understand the full dynamic of this system of product development and human development, we must underscore that imagination comes first, and that creativity and innovation are born out of it.

Nothing exists in a vacuum.

Then there was also the more prosaic boulder in the way of making progress from imagination to innovation—the misuse of the word for lucrative ends. Suddenly, imagination could be borrowed: if you wore certain jeans, you were imaginative; if you drank a certain type of bottled water or if you watched a specific TV show, you were labeled as imaginative. Others took care of imagination: they produced ever-improved means of communication, fashions, and entertainment. Few of those who bought these innovations wholesale noticed the scornful cynicism implicit in this transaction; namely, that you, the consumer, had no imagination: therefore it could be sold to you in a briefly popular form, bound to have a very short life, so that you would always buy more of it.

Against all this, my colleagues and I did well. Today, which in our fast-forward scenario is the year 2020, let's imagine that what we know is connected to how we know, that well-being is fully recognized as a predictor of success and that it's practically synonymous with this century's new education. Dr. Madeleine Holzer specifies in the noteworthy position paper "Capacities for Imaginative Learning" and related documents that it is still, to this day, our duty to gently point out that imagination and its relationship to creativity and innovation must be taught so that it might transcend the boundaries of the school. It must be a part of one's lifelong, spontaneous, habits of mind. How else, regardless of how fine and extensive our education may be, will we ever step into the shoes of someone who lives a very different life thousands of miles across the globe?

Imagination is not a conclusion: it is the springboard from which we reach for conclusions. Basking in the privileges of the developed world, we feel sorry for those who live in the strife of the developing world, but sorry is not good enough. Returning to my point from the beginning of this essay, we all must be at the wheel. That is the aesthetic beauty of the wheel; it moves us forward and connects us together. Whether it seems too onerous or not, we have no choice if we wish to survive. We cannot just be sorry; we must effect radical changes—and even that isn't enough. You see, we have to understand how to effect changes without hurting those whom we wish to help in the process. To put it simply and bluntly: imagination is empathy of the deepest kind. Ah, those extraordinary two words embodying the question mark of human intelligence and aspirations—*What if . . . ?*—to see things as if they could be otherwise. As educational philosopher Maxine Greene has said, "You cannot become that which you did not imagine."

What if we ceased to behave as if globalization were only good for the investment market and learned that all new ideas will be generated through diversity? What if we ceased to use all the social media tools to hide behind superficial information, while revealing nothing about our true selves? What if we ceased to be shortsighted and modified our political and economic behavior so that it didn't merely benefit our prestige and our wallets today, but bore fruit for all a hundred years from now?

But, you might say, if we did, well, why do all the problems still exist in 2020? Why are there still those who refuse to imagine a better world? Why are we beset by famine, wars, exploitation, destruction of the ozone? Imagining things as if they could be otherwise is its own reward, not an opiate.

The answer is painfully simple: ideas take time to ripen. It took over two thousand years for *imagination* to cease being an unwelcome word, and if you think that is a long time, consider that it took some ten thousand years for humanity to invent democracy and condemn slavery.

We cannot wait another ten thousand years, or even a thousand, for the changes necessary to allow us all to enjoy the basics of life: peace, education, material comfort, and spiritual knowledge. What, then, will speed us toward the end of the tunnel?

I have come to believe that, in the end, while visionaries and great leaders are indispensable to the growth of societies, it is that poorly defined entity to which we seldom give credit that will save us. It's the entity for whom composer Aaron Copland, in the twentieth century, composed a sonorous and noble musical salute. He called his work *Fanfare for the Common Man*. I'll adjust that a bit:

I believe in the common men and women. The seed of positive imagination is in every one of us from birth. It must be nurtured until it yields clarity of vision, born out of empathy. I look toward 2050 with hope.

I wish to thank Christopher St. Clair for his steadfast and capable assistance in writing this essay.

THE EVOLUTION OF LEADERSHIP CONSCIOUSNESS THROUGH 2020

JEFFERSON CANN

Jefferson Cann has been involved in leadership development at the individual, team, and organizational levels for the past ten years, following a successful twenty-year career in industry. He is cofounder of Extraordinary Leadership and coauthor of *An Introduction to 3-Dimensional Leadership* with Nigel Linacre. The cornerstone of his work is "self-leadership," rooted in deep connection with one's personal truth and purpose. From this, a new vision of leadership for the new world emerges.

■ ■ ■

How will the evolution of humanity's consciousness be reflected in leadership practice? How will the aims of leadership evolve, and what will leadership look like in the new "global" world?

All leadership takes place in the three dimensions of leadership—time, space, and being.[1]* As humanity's capacities evolve over the coming decades, leaders' perspectives in all these dimensions will change.

LEADERSHIP IN TIME

Presence in the Now

All leadership involves the journey from a known past and present along a path to a desired future. Changes will take place at all three points—past, present, and future—within this dimension of leadership time.

The "knowing of the present" will deepen as the discoveries of the new science, especially in neurophysiology, neuropsychology, and subatomic

---

*The author would like to acknowledge the role of Nigel Linacre, cofounder of Extraordinary Leadership, in the development of these ideas.

physics, become increasingly well-known and understood. These discoveries will illuminate afresh for new generations the ancient truths of the connectedness of all things.

This deepening of connection with the present will coincide with the growing capacity for consciousness in the new generations. This is evident already, not only in the "indigo children," but also in the changing attitudes of those entering the employment market in recent years. Younger workers bring with them a greater sense of self-value, a need to understand the purpose and implications of the work they do, a refusal to blindly do things that violate their values, less fear of insecurity, and a greater drive to put self-actualization before material wealth (e.g., lifestyle before money).

The leader's awareness of the present moment will go beyond the material facts and instinctive needs that have driven commercial society to this point. She will connect with deeper purpose and the higher energy, enabling that to transform self, others, and the situation—so that the greater harmony can emerge. She will act in the knowledge that the moment is the point of the true co-creation of reality, the point at which the potential of all that has been is realized in the flow of the eternal present.

The Nature of the Path

This deeper connection with the present will continue moment to moment—sensing the impact of each action within the constant shift of circumstance, reaction, and response in the closer and further environment. Progress along the path is no longer a process of overcoming "obstacles" in pursuit of a fixed, predefined goal, a process of fighting the competing demands of the external world as we impose our will on it. Progress becomes an exercise in "harmonic sensing" of the surrounding circumstances and forces, from the people to the events to the environment at the highest level of complexity accessible to the individual.

The essence of the journey becomes the achievement of harmony, finding not so much the path of least resistance, but a constant move along the path of greatest benefit, indicated by the degree of harmonic resonance with all that is connected with each action in each moment. Of course, this has implications for how the goal is defined.

Desired Futures

The desired future is that which, at any moment, is perceived to provide the greatest benefit for the population in question in greatest harmony with maximum benefit for the whole.* Time future as well as time past is contained in time present. The deeper the connection with time present, the greater the awareness of the dynamics of the forces at play, the greater the understanding of the effects of an action within that dynamic matrix. This means that the leader develops an increasing prescience, which enables her to maintain perception of the evolving goal within the shift of flowing events. It is the *purpose* of the greater harmony and good, not the achievement of a specific goal, that drives her.

The courage of the future leader will be based not on the ability to face and overcome obstacles, but on the ability to live what you believe to be true, knowing that the living of it will change that truth through experience and knowledge.

LEADERSHIP IN SPACE

Self-Leadership

To lead others into the future, you must first lead yourself. If you cannot lead yourself, you cannot lead anything—you can react to events, but you cannot shape them; therefore, you cannot lead. As an effective self-leader you are able to "keep your head when all about you are losing theirs and blaming it on you."[2] Self-leadership requires the ability to lead in all four of the human faculties—physical, mental, emotional, and spiritual.

---

*One example of this may be the work undertaken by Nelson Mandela immediately after his 1994 election in South Africa to ensure that the whole country, including the African National Congress (ANC), supported the national Springbok rugby team—the despised, ultimate symbol of white supremacy—at the 1995 Rugby World Cup just two years after the fall of apartheid (the focus of *Invictus,* the 2009 biopic directed by Clint Eastwood).

Physical Leadership is the ability to manage your physical state, to be able to move from a state of potential stress or fear to a state of dynamic relaxation, or flow, for optimal performance.

Mental Leadership is the ability to remain clear-sighted and rational without losing the ability to connect at the human level for the benefit of the greater good.

Emotional Leadership is the ability to acknowledge your emotional reactions, understand their purpose, and integrate them into emotionally intelligent, adult-to-adult interactions in all circumstances, rooted in the present, without regret for the past or fear for the future.

Spiritual Leadership is knowing the purpose of your actions, and how this purpose fulfills your personal sense of meaning and that of others your actions affect, from family to team to world.

Rooted in their connected present, these abilities will be the accepted core of the leaders of the future.

Leading Others

Based on their self-leadership in the four faculties, the leaders of the future will be adept in emotional intelligence, the ability to maintain "I'm okay, you're okay," adult-to-adult interactions; the social psychology of leadership; and the authenticity of knowing and living their values with compassion and integrity. What distinguishes them from many of the leaders of the past will be their purpose—the end that these abilities serve. As discussed earlier, the deep connection of the future leader intrinsically focuses him on the harmonic realization of the common good, rooted in his perception of the whole. Until now, this has not been the case.

In the past, the role of the CEO and senior management team was to ensure continued profit and shareholder value at the expense of the competition, regardless of the long-term consequences. This is now changing as the new consciousness is manifesting in the broader social sphere. In the commercial sphere, for example, no public company can now survive without a corporate social responsibility (CSR) program.

For some companies, CSR is an integral part of their corporate purpose and identity. For others, it is a small inconvenience to which they pay lip service with a minimal payment or recycling policy. Either way, in our current world all CSR activity takes place within the overall ethos of competitive consumption and growth, with all its attendant fear and aggression.

As leadership consciousness develops, the *we*, for the good of which the leader works, expands to include the broader current community, the world, and, eventually, the perceivable universe. Serving the larger world becomes intrinsic to the act of leadership at any level.

Leading in the World

We now have the Internet and the growing awareness of the global consciousness the Internet's existence signals. The ability to remain restricted in one's reality and interests requires a conscious act of perceptual restriction for more and more of the world's population. Strict socially and morally dogmatic systems are being exposed to alternatives, with predictable defensive, fear-based reactions. Limited belief systems and social codes are crumbling under the impact of unavoidable relativity.

The space opened up by the falling of these walls is terrifying for some, a gift for others. The interconnectedness of all things is increasingly demonstrated in science, spirituality, philosophy, and the events of the physical world. As this is understood by more and more of the population within the growing awareness of the redundancy of a growth economy within a finite environment, the predominant mentality will shift from one of scarcity in abundance to sufficiency within limited physical resources. This, in turn, will reduce competitive fear and aggression, allowing the shift to harmonious, connected leadership to accelerate the evolutionary shift at the global level.

"Leading the world" will then be an intrinsic part of every act of leadership at any other level as the effects of actions at the individual and group levels on the wider context will be perceived and considered. Serving self and serving the greater good in the world become one.

LEADERSHIP BEING AND THE
ACT OF LEADERSHIP

Leaders do things, and enable others to do things. Most importantly, leaders do and enable other people to do things that have never been done before in circumstances that have never previously existed. In other words, leaders act, and ACT stands for Awareness, Connection, and Transformation.

The leader is aware of and connected to himself, to those whom he leads, and with the situation he and they find themselves in. The quality of his awareness and connection determines the level of transformation that can occur—through and for the mutual benefit of all involved. Improving the quality of awareness and connection itself transforms the relationships involved. This also means that the impact of the *intentional* transformation of the leader is both greater than and more harmonious with the wider sphere.

As human consciousness evolves, the quality of leaders' vision will be measured in the future not by the degree to which it "wins" for themselves and their organization, but by the degree and breadth of harmony within the wider sphere—the degree to which it "wins" for the integrated matrix of perceived existence.*

Leaders will ACT increasingly in the moment—becoming more completely aware of all that *is* in all perceivable dimensions, thereby allowing the higher qualities to transform self, others, and the situation in harmonious relationship.

LEADERSHIP CONSCIOUSNESS

Future leaders will understand that we are all unique manifestations of whatever we think we are a manifestation of. Our purpose is to give of that uniqueness to the whole. We can do this by living what we believe

---

*Polly Higgins, the environmental lawyer, has pointed out that the legal basis for this change of perception exists in the transition from the property law that predominates today to trusteeship law. See www.pollyhiggins.com.

to be true, knowing that the living of it will change that truth as we go. To live what we believe to be true requires the continual recognition and removal of self-oriented, unnecessary, diminishing fears of the body and socially created personality that block growth—that is, the exploration of our truth. This is continual Awareness and Connection leading to continual, evolutionary Transformation.

By removing the fears of the ego/personality as we ACT, we increasingly harmonize ourselves with the whole through the unique entity of our being. As our "note" rings more true, we find our true harmonic and place within the whole. This allows the energy of the absolute/the universe/the whole to work *through* us. From this emerges the co-creation of our particular point within the universe. This, in concert with others similarly "allowing" the same flow, allows the harmonious universe (known throughout the ages as "God's Will") to unfold.

The levels of conscious awareness, connection, and transformation discussed here cannot be learned in a systematic fashion. Our minds and our hearts can respond powerfully to the vision of such a state; our higher selves might resonate with the deep understanding that such an integrated existence is, somehow, our heritage. The growth of the capability to live from such a level is a process of evolutionary development that, on the larger scale, transcends an individual lifetime, apart from the few essential individuals in each age who are born with the capacity. Its time scale is generational. The contribution of each individual—each cell within the human organism—is to choose whether to work to be a part of that evolutionary process or not and, if the choice is "yes," to work diligently to increase their capacity to be an harmonious part of the whole with integrity and without the self-delusion of vain self-aggrandizement. This is, increasingly, the essence of self-leadership.

The personal aim of the integrated, connected leader is not to be the best, the first, the most valuable: it is not recognition or praise or the leaving of a legacy. It is not to be the most harmonious, the most aware and connected, or the most humble, contributing servant. These are facets of the isolated, self-referencing ego. The new leader is deeply rooted in her own sense of purpose, which is deeply integrated in the connections with the whole and focused on the greater good. The fears of self-concern are dissolved in the aim of growing the awareness of the role one might play to serve the harmonious development of the whole. Through experience, and trial and error, the boundaries of the lower ego self will be absorbed in the growing, harmonious presence of the flowing higher self within the greater unity. Our highest aim is to play our true role in this never-ending journey for the benefit of our children's children and the generations of the universe to come.

REFERENCES

1. Nigel Linacre and Jefferson Cann, *An Introduction to 3-Dimensional Leadership* (U.K.: Extraordinary Leadership, 2011).
2. Rudyard Kipling, "If."

IF YOU CAN DREAM IT, YOU CAN DO IT

What We Can Achieve in 2020

TOMOYO NONAKA

Tomoyo Nonaka is a Japanese television personality and business-woman. From 1993 to 1997 she was the anchorwoman for the popular business program *World Business Satellite* at TV Tokyo. In addition to working as a journalist, she has been a member of many Japanese government committees, holding for Cabinet-level office, and serving in the Ministry of Finance, the Ministry of Education, and the Ministry of Economy, Trade, and Industry. She was the CEO of SANYO Electric from 2005 to 2007.

■ ■ ■

No problem can be solved by the same level of consciousness in which it occurred.

—ALBERT EINSTEIN

I remember that in a previous book, *WorldShift 2012,* I wrote about what I did in my days as chairperson of SANYO Electric Company from 2005 to 2007. During this time, I created the new vision called "Think Gaia," which means every product and service of SANYO should be designed for the next generations and for a better future of planet Earth. From this we could make it possible to produce many products that were both industry firsts and world firsts, such as the AQUA washing machine, which can recycle water for future washes, and ENELOOP, a battery that can be recharged more than 1,800 times, even by solar energy.

Those more than twelve forward-thinking concepts were to be harvested not by massive structural changes but by making new cross-functional divisions in order to integrate each other's technologies. I named this division the "Think Gaia Incubation Platform," allowing them to have a direct line to top management; that is, to me. This was only possible by sharing the new vision as a common goal.

Since we had nearly thirty company business lines, with more than 100,000 employees worldwide, a nearly sixty-year history, and total annual sales of about $25 billion, structural reorganization and change turned out to be costly actions. I strongly believe that whatever the obstacles are, as long as the vision or goal is true and right for the life of the next generations, there is a way to be found.

Although those innovative products were selling well, the board members from investment banks were not happy with this at all. In fact, they hated the new vision. They preferred gains every quarter. They did not care about creating a better future for us all.

Unfortunately, it was the time before the "Lehman Shock" occurred (that is, before 2008), so the power of the financial sector—from investment banks—was so godly strong (actually, they seemed to believe they were gods—we have the money so we wield the power to do anything we like!). They called the new vision-based evolutional reengineering ways "naive-girlish," and they tried to stop us from making those products. In the end, the investment bankers won out. The result: the flagship Think Gaia initiative was closed down. Some analysts have kindly said that I was too far ahead of the times in doing such things, especially in the manufacturing industry, which is a male chauvinistic field.

As time went by, we all experienced the worldwide effects of the Lehman Shock. World market trends seemed to shift a bit toward green initiatives in many respects. Yet by reading the last G20 statement in Mexico, and the 2012 one in Brazil, we should perhaps not be so optimistic. They did not make any clear decision about shifting the world. So how can we, the passengers on Spaceship Earth, be awakened?

On March 11, 2011 we tragically had a great earthquake and tsunami in Tohoku, Japan. It was, I thought, a wake-up call from Mother Earth.

Through these natural calamities we were made to realize that we are not simply a living creature but a creature who is allowed to live by nature. There are not many ways to avoid natural disasters. But we can make every effort to minimize the damage to society.

Japan is the only country on this planet to be attacked twice by the atomic bomb. And the third attack was triggered by the natural disaster that occurred in Fukushima at the site of the so-called peacefully powered nuclear plant. Indeed, what peaceful energy usage! Unfortunately, the fact of the matter was that it could not be of any peaceful use at all. We could not stop the radiation emissions nor eliminate them (and some radiation half-life periods are nearly 4,500 million years!). The Fukushima nuclear plant has been emitting 1000–7000 Bq (becquerel)/hour even today, as I write, after more than fifteen months have passed.

Although the Japanese government declared the Fukushima nuclear accident over, nobody really believed this. To me, the government's efforts seem to have barely begun to start to deal with the accident. The government, as well as the KEIDANREN (the Federation of Economic Organizations in Japan), did not try to shift their energy strategies in our country even after this tragic accident. I can hardly believe it. Do we need another nuclear power plant disaster to awaken from the nightmare? It is not so much a horror story but a horror reality.

During the time I was chairperson of SANYO, I was also the chair of the All Japan Photovoltaic Association. I know how excellent and profoundly cutting-edge are the technologies we have in our country. Not only the photovoltaic-plus batteries, but also so many technologies concerning the renewable energy field, as well other materials that are entirely in our hands. Yes, H_2 (hydrogen) technologies are also the world-class standard. Can you imagine if, all you had to do was water your car to drive, just like watering a plant with a watering can? It is not a dream at all anymore.

It is to be our mission, I believe, to show the people of the world that we human beings can live without nuclear or fossil fuel. Energy is the issue that dominates the way of life in the future.

Today, the Japanese government seems to be paralyzed at the

riverbank of the Jurassic Park of the twentieth century. We should cross the river toward the future side, where the rich fragrance of the soil without the nuclear plant lies. We have known this for a long time. What Japan needs to do is to shift its energy policy. I know that, once we state a true and good new vision to share with a strong leadership, we can bring that vision to fruition.

What can we achieve by 2020? The answer is totally up to us and how eagerly we want to achieve this. If you can dream it, you can do it! This is one of my favorite phrases when it comes to solving the problems in this world.

I am looking forward to seeing you in good health with a big smile in the year 2020.

THOUGHTS ON THE DAWN
OF THE AKASHIC AGE

The vision articulated in this book suggests that humanity will rise to the challenges of monumental change and bring forth the paradigms that will lead us to a more sustainable and harmonious future—to the dawn of the Akashic Age. Innovative changes in our social, economic, political, and technological systems will develop parallel to a holistic and integral worldview and integral consciousness. Our physical sciences will reflect our rising spiritual growth. This crucial shift will move us closer to the understanding that humanity has a significant role within a much larger, living cosmos.

The level of change required for the planet to shift toward a sustainable, harmonious, and more equitable future calls for us—awakening humanity—to draw on all our physical, creative, and visionary capacities. This is no sudden call; we have been forewarned. Our human systems and our worldviews have been undergoing preparation for some time for the transition to a global paradigm. A new era of social organization, communication, and understanding has been unfolding during the twenty-first century as the old systems reached their peak and began to decline.

Our modern sense of self-awareness and our physical/emotional/spiritual self have evolved to root us in a social world—a world of extended relations and social connectivity. We have been preparing ourselves for the coming of an Akashic Age.

Humanity can be said to be hardwired to evolve into an extended self—diversity within unity. Our diversity is strengthened through our connections, collaborations, and shared consciousness. Our unity is enhanced through our empathy, compassion, and shared sense of responsibility and destiny. We are responding today to an unprecedented flow of energy, information, and consciousness in and through our environment. Such intense range of impacts is catalyzing new patterns of thinking and perceptions. We are moving toward a restructuring of our inner psychological states as well as our external social structures. A new awareness in human consciousness is being birthed, driving through our social systems from the very center of our being. New organizational patterns are emerging, and with them a new form of consciousness: an Akashic consciousness.

We are now called upon to reevaluate how we see ourselves, not only within our local and global environments, but also in a grander, cosmological sense. Does the human evolutionary journey have meaning? What are our responsibilities for now and for the generations to come?

As we begin to rethink and redesign new ways and modes of interpersonal relations and communications, we begin to co-create a shared future. For the first time in our history as a human species, we will be making a conscious decision to create a shared future for ourselves as members of a planetary society.

This monumental step signifies a renewed understanding of our values, empathy, and respect. As a global family, we have deeply suffered from egocentric systems and a world driven by power and greed. These systems no longer have the power, or the mandate, to take us into a sustainable and harmonious future. The years of transitional change are already upon us and signify a period of time in which many of the seeds already planted will sprout and develop around the world—in projects, communities, social networks, and organizations.

The new-paradigm Akashic models are not likely to emerge from the center—like the Medici-influenced Renaissance of the Late Middle Ages—but rather from a groundswell of people-centered change. The new renaissance will come from the periphery and from the bottom up. It will be a distributed and networked emergence of conscious individuals and groupings. Like ink dots on blotting paper, these conscious and creative focal points will spread their influence until the time when the ink dots begin to change the color of the blotting paper. The social change now emerging is springing from the hearts, spirit, and consciousness of the people.

Out of the epiphany of awakening will come the increased sense, and inner desire, to develop humanitarian, ecological, and equitable systems. It often happens that an awakening in consciousness rouses the need to get involved in service for a common purpose, based on an awareness that each of us is ultimately entangled with all others within the web of life. What we choose to do today will be inherited by the world to come. We each thus have an obligation to foster a more integral, empathic, and sustainable world.

The transition into a planetary epoch that is sustainable and equitable requires a heightened sense of moral and ethical responsibility and an increase in creativity. We are being called on to respond differently to the world around us—not in fear or apprehension, but with robustness and a positive focus. We have to respect that the world in which we live is a living system in which we are an integral and essential element.

The world we are moving into requires of us that we both inspire and be inspired. Our scope for shared compassion, consciousness, and collective intention has to be brought to bear on our future societies, our communities, and our entire global civilization. The time to pretend that we are still adolescents is over.

We also require an individual human (r)evolution. That is, a shift away from being absorbed in petty thoughts of a separate individuality and ego to a recognition that as individuals we have an inherent connection with all life in the cosmos. We must therefore redefine—or refine—our own lives through this renewal of understanding. To participate in co-creating our future requires that we maintain balance and harmony between the world outside us and the world within us. That is, we must find a balance between social engagement, responsibility to our families and community, and the development of our own self. We cannot be overwhelmed by the external impacts and obligations of our lives. Within the tumult of change and transformation, we must remain balanced and focused.

We should be careful not to underestimate, or be complacent in the face of, the degree of fundamental and unprecedented change that is now upon us. As a species we are shifting into a more integral and primary relationship with the larger fabric of life.

This period of (r)evolutionary change requires a qualitative transformation in our consciousness. We do not need to wield physical or political power to be effective agents of this transformation. We each can learn to expand and refine our ways of perception, thinking, and action. The qualitative transformation of our global civilization can only come about through a (r)evolution in our consciousness.

Aspects of an evolving consciousness suggest an empathic mind that is aware of its connectivity both locally and globally, physically as well as nonphysically. The new sciences, as described in this book, validate the underlying coherence of the universe. The new Akashic paradigm recognizes that the coherence of the whole is a precondition of the functioning of the parts. It is important to recognize that coherence is not merely an individual attribute. The right way to be and to act is not just to enhance our own, individual coherence, but to contribute to the coherence of the systems that frame and sustain our life. This means achieving or safeguarding our coherence with our fellows in a community, in a state and nation, in a culture, and in the living world as a whole. This way of behaving supports the precepts of a quantum resonance–based, nonlocal consciousness—an Akashic consciousness.

A state of consciousness that reflects diversity within unity develops through human activity that expresses both greater individuation and a greater sense of shared responsibility. It is time to view our situation through the wide-angle lens of wisdom: we need to begin to see, understand, and act on the bigger picture. Shortsighted thinking must be relegated to the past, for there is no time left for poor decisions.

Recognizing the bigger picture, and the central importance of coherence, is a key to our individual health and well-being, as well as to the survival of our species. The Akashic paradigm gives us a coherent view of ourselves, of nature, and of the cosmos. Our capacity for making the needed changes at this critical moment equips our species with the potential to solve our current and future problems. We are about to see a profound change in the tenor of human life on this planet. Everything we do today is about this monumental change leading toward an Akashic Age. There is no greater responsibility and no greater accomplishment than doing our best to make it happen.

NOTES

CHAPTER 3. DILEMMAS AT THE TURNING POINT

1. Thompson, *Transforming History*, 14.
2. Morris, *Why the West Rules—For Now*, 590.
3. Tainter, *The Collapse of Complex Societies*.
4. Heinberg, *The End to Growth*, 136–37.
5. "Why Is 'Food Security' Sparking Unrest?"
6. Booth, *Theory of World Security*.
7. Dixon, *Futurewise*, 71.
8. Heinberg, *The End to Growth*, 129.
9. Gallopin, Hammond, Raskin, and Swart, "Branch Points."
10. Williams, "The Future of Global Systems," 15–16.

CHAPTER 7. NEW AKASHIC MODELS

1. Rifkin, *The Third Industrial Revolution*, 172.
2. Henderson, *Ethical Markets*, 17.
3. Laughlin, *Powering the Future*, 92.
4. Ibid., 92.
5. Rifkin, *The Third Industrial Revolution*, 40.
6. Kaku, *Physics of the Future*, 214.
7. Henderson, *Ethical Markets*, 63.
8. Diamandis and Kotler, *Abundance*, 176.

CHAPTER 9. THE PILLARS OF A
NEW CONSCIOUSNESS

1. Cited in Atwater, *Beyond the Indigo Children,* 134.

2. Strauss and Howe, *Millennials Rising.*

3. Cited in Carroll and Tober, *The Indigo Children 10 Years Later,* 86.

4. Ibid., 123.

BIBLIOGRAPHY

Atwater, Phyllis Marie. *Beyond the Indigo Children: The New Children and the Coming of the Fifth World*. Rochester, Vt.: Bear & Company, 2005.

Booth, Ken. *Theory of World Security*. Cambridge, U.K.: Cambridge University Press, 2007.

Carroll, Lee, and Jan Tober. *The Indigo Children 10 Years Later*. London: Hay House, 2009.

Diamandis, Peter, and Steven Kotler. *Abundance: The Future Is Better Than You Think*. New York: Free Press, 2012.

Dixon, Patrick. *Futurewise: Six Faces of Global Change*. London: Profile Books, 2007.

Gallopin, G. H., A. Hammond, P. Raskin, and R. Swart. "Branch Points: Global Scenarios and Human Choice." Stockholm Environment Institute—Global Scenario Group, 1997.

Heinberg, Richard. *The End to Growth: Adapting to Our New Economic Reality*. Forest Row, U.K.: Clairview, 2011.

Henderson, Hazel. *Ethical Markets: Growing the Green Economy*. White River Junction, Vt.: Chelsea Green Publishing Company, 2006.

Kaku, Michio. *Physics of the Future: How Science Will Shape Human Destiny and Our Daily Lives by the Year 2100*. New York: Doubleday, 2011.

Laughlin, Robert. *Powering the Future: How We Will (Eventually) Solve the Energy Crisis and Fuel the Civilization of Tomorrow*. New York: Basic Books, 2011.

Morris, Ian. *Why the West Rules—For Now*. London: Profile Books, 2011.

Rifkin, Jeremy. *The Third Industrial Revolution*. London: Palgrave Macmillan, 2011.

Strauss, William, and Neil Howe. *Millennials Rising: The Next Great Generation*. New York: Vintage, 2000.

Tainter, Joseph. *The Collapse of Complex Societies*. New York: Cambridge University Press, 1988.

Thompson, William Irwin. *Transforming History: A New Curriculum for a Planetary Culture*. Great Barrington, Mass.: Lindisfarne Books, 2009.

"Why Is 'Food Security' Sparking Unrest?" http://edition.cnn.com/2010/ BUSINESS/09/22/un.food.security.poverty/index.html. Accessed January 11, 2013.

Williams, Phil. "The Future of Global Systems: Collapse or Resilience?" Strategic Studies Institute, 2008.

RECOMMENDED READING

GLOBAL TRANSFORMATION

Benkler, Yochai. *The Penguin and the Leviathan: The Triumph of Cooperation over Self-Interest*. New York: Crown Business, 2011.

Bok, Derek. *The Politics of Happiness: What Government Can Learn from the New Research on Well-Being*. Princeton, N.J.: Princeton University Press, 2010.

Christi, Nicolya. *2012: A Clarion Call: Your Soul's Purpose in Conscious Evolution*. Rochester, Vt.: Inner Traditions, 2011.

Dennis, Kingsley. *New Revolutions for a Small Planet*. London: Watkins, 2012.

Elgin, Duane. *Awakening Earth: Exploring the Evolution of Human Culture and Consciousness*. New York: William Morrow & Company, 1993.

———. *Promise Ahead: A Vision of Hope and Action for Humanity's Future*. New York: William Morrow, 2000.

———. *The Living Universe*. San Francisco: Berrett-Koehler Publishers, 2009.

Hawken, Paul. *Blessed Unrest: How the Largest Social Movement in the World Is Restoring Grace, Justice and Beauty to the World*. London: Penguin, 2008.

Kelly, Sean. *Coming Home: The Birth & Transformation of the Planetary Era*. Great Barrington, Mass.: Lindisfarne Books, 2010.

Korten, David. *The Great Turning: From Empire to Earth Community*. San Francisco: Berrett-Koehler, 2007.

Laszlo, Ervin. *The Chaos Point: The World at the Crossroads*. Charlottesville, Va.: Hampton Roads, 2006.

———. *Quantum Shift in the Global Brain*. Rochester, Vt.: Inner Traditions, 2008.

———. *Worldshift 2012: Making Green Business, New Politics, and Higher Consciousness Work Together*. Rochester, Vt.: Inner Traditions, 2009.

Laszlo, Ervin, and Jude Currivan. *Cosmos: A Co-Creator's Guide to the Whole World*. London: Hay House, 2008.

Macy, Joanna. *Active Hope: How to Face the Mess We're In without Going Crazy*. Novato, Calif.: New World Library, 2012.

Morris, Ian. *Why the West Rules—For Now*. London: Profile Books, 2011.

Novak, Martin. *Supercooperators: Beyond the Survival of the Fittest: Why Cooperation, Not Competition, Is the Key to Life*. Edinburgh: Canongate Books, 2012.

Russell, Peter. *The Global Brain: The Awakening Earth in a New Century*. Edinburgh: Floris Books, 2007.

———. *Waking Up in Time: Our Future Evolution and the Meaning of Now*. Llandeilo, Carmarthenshire: Cygnus Books, 2009.

Strauss, William, and Neil Howe. *Millennials Rising: The Next Great Generation*. New York: Vintage, 2000.

Wheatley, Margaret, and Deborah Frieze. *Walk Out Walk On: A Learning Journey into Communities Daring to Live the Future Now*. San Francisco: Berrett-Koehler, 2011.

NEW CONSCIOUSNESS

De Bono, Edward. *New Thinking for the New Millenium*. London: Penguin, 2000.

Dennis, Kingsley. *New Consciousness for a New World*. Rochester, Vt.: Inner Traditions, 2011.

———. *The Struggle for Your Mind*. Rochester, Vt.: Inner Traditions, 2012.

Gardner, Howard. *Five Minds for the Future*. Boston: Harvard Business School Press, 2009.

Gebser, Jean. *The Ever-Present Origin: The Foundations and Manifestations of the Aperspectival World*. Columbus: Ohio University Press, 1986.

Harman, Willis. *Global Mind Change: The Promise of the 21st Century*. San Francisco: Berrett-Koehler, 1998.

Kahneman, Daniel. *Thinking, Fast and Slow*. London: Penguin, 2012.

Laszlo, Ervin, Stanislav Grof, and Peter Russell. *The Consciousness Revolution*. Shaftesbury, Dorset, U.K.: Element Books, 1999.

McGilchrist, Ian. *The Master and His Emissary: The Divided Brain and the Making of the Western World*. New Haven, Conn.: Yale University Press, 2009.

Ornstein, Robert, and Paul Ehrlich. *New World, New Mind.* Cambridge, Mass.: ISHK, 2000.

Ring, Kenneth. *The Omega Project: Near-Death Experiences, UFO Encounters, and Mind at Large.* New York: William Morrow, 1992.

Salk, Jonas. *The Survival of the Wisest.* New York: Harper & Row, 1973.

NEW ECONOMICS

Daly, Herman. *Beyond Growth: Economics of Sustainable Development.* Boston: Beacon Press, 1997.

Douthwaite, Richard. *The Ecology of Money.* Totnes, U.K.: Green Books, 2000.

Eisenstein, Charles. *Sacred Economics: Money, Gift, and Society in the Age of Transition.* New York: Evolver Editions, 2011.

Greco, Thomas, H. *The End of Money and the Future of Civilization.* Edinburgh: Floris Books, 2010.

Greer, John Michael. *Wealth of Nature: Economics As If Survival Matters.* Gabriola Island, B.C.: New Society Publishers, 2011.

Hallsmith, Gwendolyn, and Bernard Lietaer. *Creating Wealth: Growing Local Economies with Local Currencies.* Gabriola Island, B.C.: New Society Publishers, 2011.

Hawken, Paul, Amory Lovins, and L. Hunter Lovins. *Natural Capitalism: The Next Industrial Revolution,* 10th anniversary ed. New York: Routledge, 2005.

Heinberg, Richard. *The End to Growth: Adapting to Our New Economic Reality.* Forest Row, U.K.: Clairview, 2011.

Jackson, Tim. *Prosperity without Growth: Economics for a Finite Planet.* London: Routledge, 2011.

Kent, Deirdre. *Healthy Money, Healthy Planet: Developing Sustainability through New Money Systems.* Nelson, N.Z.: Craig Potton Publishing, 2005.

Lietaer, Bernard, and Stephen Belgin. *New Money for a New World.* Denver: Qiterra Press, 2011.

Schumacher, Ernst Friedrich. *Small Is Beautiful: A Study of Economics As If People Mattered.* London: Vintage, 2011.

Shuman, Michael. *Local Dollars, Local Sense: How to Shift Your Money from Wall Street to Main Street and Achieve Real Prosperity.* White River Junction, Vt.: Chelsea Green Publishing Company, 2012.

NEW SCIENCES

Chilton Pearce, Joseph. *The Biology of Transcendence: A Blueprint of the Human Spirit.* Rochester, Vt.: Park Street Press, 2004.

———. *Heart-Mind Matrix: How the Heart Can Teach the Mind New Ways to Think.* Rochester, Vt.: Park Street Press, 2012.

Citro, Massimo. *The Basic Code of the Universe: The Science of the Invisible in Physics, Medicine, and Spirituality.* Rochester, Vt.: Park Street Press, 2011.

Ho, Mae Wan. *The Rainbow and the Worm: The Physics of Organisms.* Singapore: World Scientific, 1998.

Laszlo, Ervin. *Science and the Akashic Field.* Rochester, Vt.: Inner Traditions, 2004.

———. *The Akasha Paradigm: Revolution in Science; Evolution in Consciousness.* Cardiff, Calif.: Waterside Publications, 2012.

Laszlo, Ervin, and Kingsley Dennis, eds. *The New Science & Spirituality Reader.* Rochester, Vt.: Inner Traditions, 2012.

Lipton, Bruce. *The Biology of Belief: Unleashing the Power of Consciousness, Matter and Miracles.* Carlsbad, Calif.: Hay House Inc., 2008.

McFadden, Johnjoe. *Quantum Evolution: Life in the Multiverse.* London: Flamingo, 2000.

Narby, Jeremy. *Intelligence in Nature.* London: Jeremy P. Tarcher, 2006.

Nielsen, Michael. *Reinventing Discovery: The New Era of Networked Science.* Princeton, N.J.: Princeton University Press, 2011.

Sheldrake, Rupert. *Morphic Resonance: The Nature of Formative Causation.* Rochester, Vt.: Park Street Press, 2009.

Siegel, Daniel. *Mindsight: Transform Your Brain with the New Science of Kindness.* Oxford, U.K.: Oneworld Publications, 2010.

Talbot, Michael. *The Holographic Universe.* London: HarperCollins, 1996.

STATE OF THE WORLD

Brown, Lester. *World on the Edge: How to Prevent Environmental and Economic Collapse.* New York: Routledge, 2011.

Farnish, Keith. *Time's Up: An Uncivilized Solution to a Global Crisis.* Totnes, U.K.: Green Books, 2009.

Greer, John Michael. *The Long Descent: A User's Guide to the End of the Industrial Age.* Gabriola Island, B.C.: New Society Publishers, 2008.

Homer-Dixon, Thomas. *The Upside of Down: Catastrophe, Creativity, and the Renewal of Civilization*. New York: Island Press, 2006.

Meadows, Donella H., Jorgen Randers, and Dennis L. Meadows. *The Limits to Growth: The 30-year Update*. London: Routledge, 2004.

Orlov, Dmitry. *Reinventing Collapse: The Soviet Experience & American Prospects*. Gabriola Island, B.C.: New Society Publishers, 2011.

Ornstein, Robert, and Paul Ehrlich. *Humanity on a Tightrope*. Lanham, Md.: Rowman & Littlefield Publishers, 2010.

Rubin, Jeff. *Why Your World Is About to Get a Whole Lot Smaller: Oil and the End of Globalisation*. London: Virgin Books, 2010.

Wu, Timothy. *The Master Switch: The Rise and Fall of Information Empires*. New York: Atlantic Books, 2010.

SUSTAINABILITY

Astyk, Sharon. *Depletion and Abundance: Life on the New Home Front*. Gabriola Island, B.C.: New Society Publishers, 2008.

Berry, Thomas. *The Great Work: Our Way into the Future*. New York: Three Rivers Press, 1999.

Capra, Fritjof. *The Hidden Connections: A Science for Sustainable Living*. New York: Flamingo, 2010.

Heinberg, Richard, and Daniel Lerch. *Post Carbon Reader: Managing the 21st Century's Sustainability Crisis*. Berkeley: University of California Press, 2010.

Henderson, Hazel, and Daisaku Ikeda. *Planetary Citizenship: Your Values, Beliefs and Actions Can Shape a Sustainable World*. Santa Monica, Calif.: Middleway Press, 2004.

Hopkins, Rob. *The Transition Handbook: From Oil Dependency to Local Resilience* (Transition Guides). Totnes, U.K.: Green Books, 2008.

————. *The Transition Companion: Making Your Community More Resilient in Uncertain Times* (Transition Guides). Totnes, U.K.: Transition Books, 2011.

Laszlo, Ervin, and Allen Combs. *Thomas Berry, Dreamer of the Earth: The Spiritual Ecology of the Father of Environmentalism*. Rochester, Vt.: Inner Traditions, 2011.

MacKay, David. *Sustainable Energy—Without the Hot Air*. Cambridge, U.K.: UIT, 2008.

Martenson, Chris. *The Crash Course: The Unsustainable Future of Our Economy, Energy, and Environment*. New York: John Wiley & Sons, 2011.

McKibben, Bill. *Eaarth: Making a Life on a Tough New Planet*. New York: St. Martin's/Griffin, 2011.

Willis, Rebecca, Molly Webb, and James Wilsdon. *The Disrupters: Lessons for Low-Carbon Innovation from the New Wave of Environmental Pioneers*. London: Nesta, 2007.

WORLD FUTURES

Clarke, Arthur C. *Profiles of the Future,* 2nd rev. ed. London: Indigo, 2000.

Dennis, Kingsley, and John Urry. *After the Car*. Cambridge, U.K.: Polity Press, 2009.

Diamandis, Peter, and Steven Kotler. *Abundance: The Future Is Better Than You Think*. New York: Free Press, 2012.

Dixon, Patrick. *Futurewise: Six Faces of Global Change*. London: Profile Books, 2007.

Greer, John Michael. *The Ecotechnic Future: Envisioning a Post-Peak World*. Gabriola Island, B.C.: New Society Publishers, 2009.

Kaku, Michio. *Physics of the Future: How Science Will Shape Human Destiny and Our Daily Lives by the Year 2100*. New York: Doubleday, 2011.

Lovins, Amory. *Reinventing Fire: Bold Business Solutions for the New Energy Era*. White River Junction, Vt.: Chelsea Green Publishing Company, 2011.

Randers, Jorgen. *2052: A Global Forecast for the Next Forty Years*. White River Junction Vt.: Chelsea Green Publishing Company, 2012.

Rifkin, Jeremy. *The Empathic Civilization: The Race to Global Consciousness in a World in Crisis*. Cambridge, U.K.: Polity Press, 2010.

———. *The Third Industrial Revolution*. London: Palgrave Macmillan, 2011.

Steele, Robert David. *The Open-Source Everything Manifesto: Transparency, Truth, and Trust*. New York: Evolver Editions, 2012.

INDEX